SUMMER OF THE
SEVENTEENTH DOLL

Summer

of the

Seventeenth

Doll

A new play by

RAY LAWLER

RANDOM HOUSE

NEW YORK

To
JOHN SUMNER
who directed the play from Melbourne to London,
and to *The Australian Elizabethan Theatre Trust*
which made such a journey possible

Photographs by courtesy of Angus McBean, London

SUMMER OF THE SEVENTEENTH DOLL *was first presented in America by The Theatre Guild and The Playwrights' Company, by arrangement with The Australian Elizabethan Theatre Trust and St. James's Players, Limited, at the Coronet Theatre, New York City, on January 22, 1958, with the following cast:*

(IN ORDER OF APPEARANCE)

PEARL CUNNINGHAM	Madge Ryan
BUBBA RYAN	Fenella Maguire
OLIVE LEECH	June Jago
BARNEY IBBOT	Ray Lawler
EMMA LEECH	Ethel Gabriel
ROO WEBBER	Kenneth Warren
JOHNNIE DOWD	Richard Pratt

Directed by John Sumner

Scenery designed by Anne Fraser

and supervised by Marvin Reiss

Production Associate: Warren Caro

The entire action of the play takes place in a double-storied terrace cottage in Carlton, Victoria

ACT ONE

Scene 1 A Sunday in early December, 1952. Late afternoon
Scene 2 Next morning

ACT TWO

Scene 1 New Year's Eve
Scene 2 The following Friday evening

ACT THREE

Next morning

ACT ONE

Charming and fast-vanishing relics of Victorian architecture in Australia are the double-storied brick cottages with elaborately patterned ironwork decorating their verandas—hanging in fringes from above, and forming pale, intricate barriers down below.

These are almost invariably found in the older sections of the city, and the house of the play is situated in Carlton, a now scruffy but once fashionable suburb of Melbourne.

The setting is a composite study of a ground-floor front room, with adjacent hallway, staircase, and a passage leading to the kitchen, held between a front and a back veranda. It should be noted that, although the main scene of the action is the interior of the house, the front veranda, with a section of overgrown, palmy garden before it, should be visible either through a scrim wall or a cut-away section. This is not an essential point with the back veranda, however, which exists mainly to provide a connection with BUBBA'S *place next door.*

Narrow-leaf French windows give entrance to the room from the back veranda, and a front door lets onto the other; both verandas are profusely decorated with green shrubbery and ferns. These, together with the wildness of the garden, should make an enshrouding contrast to the interior of the house, which has a dominant note of cheerfully faded pink in its color scheme.

There is little pattern or taste evident in the furniture, ranging as it does from the heavy upright piano bought second-hand by EMMA *in 1919, to the chromium smoker's stand won by* OLIVE *in a pub raffle last month. The main decorative features are the souvenirs brought down by* ROO *on past visits.*

The most notable of these are sixteen kewpie dolls, wearing tinsel headdresses and elaborately fuzzy skirts, attached to thin black canes shaped like walking sticks. These peep coyly from behind pictures, flower in two's and three's from vases, and are crossed over the mantelpiece. They have as their companions a flight of brilliantly plumaged stuffed Northern Queensland birds, a variety of tinted coral pieces and shells from the Great Barrier Reef, and two picture frames backed with black velvet to which cling a crowd of shimmering-winged tropical butterflies.

The entire effect should be a glowing interior luminosity protected from the drabness outside by a light-filtered, shifting curtain of greenery.

ACT ONE

SCENE ONE

Time: Early December.

It is five o'clock on a warm Sunday afternoon. The room of the play has a dressed-up look that is complementary to, and yet extending beyond, the usual decorative scheme. A table is heavily set for the big meal of the week, Sunday tea.

At curtain rise, BUBBA RYAN, *a dark, shy-looking girl of twenty-two, is busily tying wide blue ribbons to two of the red-and-white-striped candies known as walking sticks. At the same time she is chatting with a touch of wistful authoritativeness to* PEARL CUNNINGHAM, *who is sitting smoking nearby on a sofa, ostensibly looking through a magazine, but listening rather suspiciously.* PEARL *is a biggish woman, well corseted, with dyed red hair. She is a widow driven back to earning a living by the one job she knows well, that of barmaid, though she would infinitely prefer something more classy—head saleswoman in a frock salon, for instance. The pub game, she feels, is rather crude. She is wearing what she refers to as her "good black," with a double string of artificial pearls. Very discreet.*

BUBBA. . . . So I was the only one went to the weddin'. August it was, and the boys were away, though of course when Olive wrote up and told them, they sent down money for a present. But I had to buy it and take it along, Olive wouldn't have anythin' to do with it. Wouldn't even help me pick anythin' out.

3

PEARL (*Questioningly*). The . . . boys . . . didn't mind her gettin' married, then?

BUBBA (*Frowning a little*). I dunno. I s'pose they did, in a way —'specially Barney, it must have been a bit of a shock to him —but like I said, they wouldn't do anythin' to stand in her way. That's how they are, see. Olive was the one really kicked up a fuss. She wouldn't believe, even up till the Saturday afternoon, that Nance'd ever go through with it.

PEARL. If you ask me, I'd say this Nancy had her head screwed on the right way.

BUBBA (*Slowly, forgetting the walking sticks for a moment*). She got tired of waiting, I think. Olive doesn't mind it, she just looks forward to the next time, but it used to get on Nance's nerves a bit. 'N', of course, she reads a lot, and this feller, this Harry Allaway—he works in a book shop, and he'd bring books into the pub for her. I s'pose that's how he got around her, really. I don't reckon Barney's ever read a book in his life.

PEARL (*Broodingly*). Mmmmm. Well, I'm fond of a good book myself now and then.

BUBBA (*Smilingly tolerant*). You won't need any till after April. Even Nancy, she only used to read in the winter. . . .
  (OLIVE's *voice, nervously importunate, calls from upstairs.*)

OLIVE. Bubba. . . .

BUBBA (*Moving up to arch*). Yes?

OLIVE. Those earrings of mine with the green stones . . .

BUBBA. Haven't seen 'em.

OLIVE. Ooh, I'll bet the old girl's taken a loan of them, she knew I wanted to . . . (*With a change of voice*) No, it's all right, here they are. Couldn't see 'em for lookin'.

(BUBBA *comes back into room, smiles at* PEARL *and speaks half apologetically.*)

BUBBA. Olive always gets nervous. We used to have to joke her out of it, Nancy and me. Only this time I think she's got it worse'n usual. I mean, she's probably worryin' a bit how you're goin' to fit in.

PEARL (*Sharply*). I don't have to fit in. What I'm here for is a . . . a visit, and if Olive's told you it's anythin' else . . .

BUBBA (*Hastily*). Oh, she hasn't. She's hardly said a word.

PEARL. In that case, then, there's no need for you to get nasty.

BUBBA (*Surprised*). I wasn't bein' nasty.

PEARL. You were. Nasty-minded. What you said before 'bout not needin' any books till after April was bad enough. It strikes me you know too much of this place for your own good.

BUBBA. I've lived next door all my life, why shouldn't I know?

PEARL. I'm not goin' to argue, you just shouldn't, that's all.

BUBBA. But you said I was bein' nasty—what made you say that? (*Under the directness of her gaze,* PEARL *shifts uneasily, not willing to implicate herself further.* BUBBA *returns to table and continues quietly*) I'll bet Olive never told you there was anythin' nasty 'bout the lay-off season.

5

PEARL (*Staring straight ahead*). That's none of your business.

OLIVE (*Offstage*). Hang on to your hats and mittens, kids, here I come again. (*She comes downstairs, wearing a crisp green-and-white summer frock. Moves with a trace of excitement into room, showing herself off*) Well, whaddya think this time? Snazzy enough? It mightn't knock your eye out, but it's nice and cool, and it's the sort of thing Roo likes. Y'know . . . fresh and green. . . .

> (*She postures, waiting for their comments. Despite a surface cynicism and thirty-seven years of age, there is something curiously unfinished about* OLIVE, *an eagerness that properly belongs to extreme youth. This is intensified at the moment by her nervous anticipation. She is a barmaid at the same city hotel as* PEARL, *but, unlike the latter, she enjoys the job.* BUBBA, *still a little unsettled by her spat with* PEARL, *blurts hastily.*)

BUBBA. Yes, it's—it's lovely.
> (OLIVE *gives a nervous laugh and embraces her.*)

OLIVE. Pearl?

PEARL (*Reluctantly*). Yes, not my taste, but it suits you.

OLIVE (*Crossing to mirror and making last-minute adjustments*). Well, it'll have to do, anyway. I haven't got time to change again. (*She turns to survey room*) Now, what else is there? I know—get the beer in!

BUBBA (*Quickly*). I'll do it.

OLIVE (*After her retreating figure*). Would yer, luv? In the fridge. God, she's a good kid, that.

PEARL. Yeh. I'd say she knows more than her prayers, just the same.

OLIVE (*Mildly astonished*). Bubba? Don't be silly, she's only a baby.

PEARL. Not too much of a baby. If Vera ever spoke to me like that, I'd put her straight back across my knee. And I don't think it's nice the way this one acts. . . .

OLIVE. How?

PEARL. Just as if she owns the place.

OLIVE. Well, whaddya expect? She's been runnin' in and out ever since she was old enough to walk. Roo and Barney she treats as if they were uncles. . . . (*She laughs suddenly, turning to shake her head at* PEARL) God, you're a wag. Talk about Cautious Kate!

PEARL. Why?

OLIVE. Look at them suitcases by the stairs! You'd think someone was gettin' ready for a moonlight flit.

PEARL (*Firmly*). That's different. I've taken my overnighter up, and I'm not taking anythin' else till I'm certain.

OLIVE. Don't be silly. I told yer, he's all right.

PEARL. Yes. Well, I'll find that out for meself, if you don't mind.

OLIVE. Oh, nobody's tryin' to talk you into anythin'. Just don't take too long to decide, that's all.

PEARL. Where's that photo you said you were gunna show me?

OLIVE. Oh, yeh. (*Collects framed enlargement from sideboard and takes it to her*) You can see him much better in this one, those others he was always clownin' about. (PEARL *takes photograph and studies it*) It's the four of us at Luna Park the year before last. Nance is on the end there.

PEARL. She looks drunk.

OLIVE. She was drunk. Right after that was taken she got sick on the Ocean Wave.

PEARL (*Nodding distastefully*). Yes. I can imagine she'd be the sort who'd get sick on an Ocean Wave.

OLIVE (*Sincerely*). She wasn't like that, really. Nance was . . . she was a real good sport. Barney was pretty fond of her.

PEARL (*Snorting*). You can see that, the way he's holdin' her. Bit intimate, isn't it?

OLIVE. Listen, luvvie, you better make up your mind. These are a coupla sugar-cane cutters fresh from the tropics—not two professors from the University.
(*She carries picture back to sideboard.*)

PEARL. I know one thing, he'll never lay hands on me like that in public.

OLIVE. Won't he? Honest, you've never met a bloke like Barney. Only about so big, and yet—I dunno—the women go mad on him.

PEARL. I'll believe it when I see it. Didn't seem to stop her goin' off and gettin' married.

OLIVE.   She made a mistake.

PEARL.   Who says?

OLIVE.   I say. Marriage is different, and Nancy knew it. Just because there was no hope of hookin' on with Barney . . .

PEARL.   Her own fault. I'll guarantee she made herself cheap. So long as a woman keeps her self-respect, any man will marry her.

OLIVE.   I wouldn't bank on that, Pearl. Not with Barney.

PEARL.   Oh, I'm not anticipatin' anythin', believe me. But from all you've said, it's about time some decent woman took this feller in hand. I don't reckon I've ever heard of anyone with more reasons to get married in all my life.

OLIVE.   Maybe I shouldna told you.

PEARL (*Darkly*).   Oh, don't worry, I would've found out. I'm a mother. A thing like that—you couldn't trick me.

OLIVE.   He'll probably tell you himself, anyway; he doesn't make any secret of it—

(BUBBA *enters quickly, her arms full of bottles of beer.*)

BUBBA.   Oh, golly, these are cold. . . .

OLIVE.   Here, let me help you.

PEARL.   Put 'em on the table and you'll get rings on the cloth.

OLIVE (*As they set out bottles at regular intervals*).   Doesn't matter. A few bottles make a party look a party, I think. (*To* BUBBA) Did you do your walkin' sticks?

9

BUBBA.   Yes, I haven't put 'em up yet.
    (*She moves to collect them.*)

PEARL.   What are they for?

OLIVE.   Tell her, Bubba.

BUBBA (*Lamely*).   Oh, they're just a bit of a joke. One's for Roo and one's for Barney.

OLIVE.   It started off the first year they came down, she was only a little thing—how old were you, Bub?

BUBBA (*As she takes walking sticks to set them up on mantelpiece*).   Five.

OLIVE.   She was always in and out here, and when Roo bought me the first lot of presents and she saw the doll among 'em, she howled her eyes out. She wanted a doll on a walkin' stick too, she said. So out the two of them go—after eight o'clock at night it was—tryin' to bang up a shop to get her one. But all they could buy were these lolly walkin' sticks, and in the end that's what they had to bring her back. Well, she was as happy as Larry; off she went to bed, one in each hand. After that they always brought 'em down every year. . . .

BUBBA.   Till I was fifteen. . . .

OLIVE.   Oh, yes, this is funny, listen. They didn't seem to wake up that she was gettin' too old for lollies, see, they kept on bringin' 'em down, bringin' 'em down, so Nancy put her up to a dodge. The year she was fifteen, when they arrived with their bundle of presents, there she had a walkin' stick for each of *them,* tied up with blue ribbons, sittin' on the mantelpiece. It taught 'em a lesson, all right. Ever since, whenever they've brought me a doll, they've always brought her down gloves, or scent, or—or somethin' like that.

(*There is a faint pause.* PEARL *is clearly unimpressed by the story, and makes little attempt to hide it.*)

PEARL.   I see.

BUBBA (*A trifle ashamed*).   I said it was only a bit of a joke. Is there anythin' else you want me to do, Ol?

OLIVE.   No, I don't think so, luv . . . but you're gunna stay and meet them, aren't yer?

BUBBA.   No, I've got to change and everythin'. I—I think I'll come in after tea.

OLIVE (*Understandingly*).   Just as you like. (*She moves to veranda with* BUBBA) What about comin' in and havin' tea with us?

BUBBA (*Anxious to escape*).   No, I'll come in after.

OLIVE.   Well, don't forget now.

BUBBA.   I won't.
   (*She has gone.* OLIVE *surveys the sky.*)

OLIVE.   It's startin' to get dark. I wonder where that mother of mine can have got to?

PEARL.   Where's she supposed to have gone?

OLIVE.   The community singin'. But that oughta been out long ago.

11

PEARL (*Consulting her watch, and rising with alarm*).   It's after six.

OLIVE (*Dashing back into room*).   Yeh. Oh, she's an old shrewdie, that one. I wouldn't mind bettin' she's gone down to the terminal to meet them. She'll get a fiver each out of them before they find a taxi.

PEARL.   You shouldn't say things like that about your mother.

OLIVE.   Listen, a fiver's nothin'. She shakes them down for all they're worth the whole time they're here. (*Switching on radio, which presently plays dreamy waltz*) 'Course they're a wake up, but they don't seem to mind. 'Fact, I think Roo likes it. (*She looks at photograph*) Good old Roo. I reckon he's got the best-lookin' mouth in the world.

PEARL (*Inspecting her make-up at mantelpiece*).   He's certainly a better proposition than the other one.

OLIVE.   Oh, but you can't compare them, they're different types. I mean, Roo's the big man of the two, but it's Barney makes you laugh. And like I said, it's Barney the women go for.

PEARL (*Aggrieved*).   I dunno why I always have to get tangled up with little men, just the same. Even Wallie, he was shorter than me. The day we got married I had to wear low heels. . . .

OLIVE.   Barney's not all that short. You wait, you'll see.

PEARL.   Yeh. Well, he'd better not start countin' on anythin', I haven't made up me mind yet. How do you reckon my hair looks?

OLIVE (*Taking a cursory glance*).   Pretty good.

12

PEARL. I don't think that new girl 'round at Rene's knows how to handle it, she doesn't seem to get down to the roots. (*Turning suddenly*) What do they call him Barney for, anyway?

OLIVE. Barney's bull, I think. His right name's Arthur.

PEARL. Oh.

OLIVE (*Enjoyably*). Did I ever tell you 'bout Roo's name? I used to think at first that it was short for Kanga, and that's what I called him once. He just looked at me silly like, and said—Kanga? Well, I said, isn't that what the Roo's part of? You should've seen him—he roared! Then he told me what Roo was, short for his real name, and just see if you can guess what that is? (PEARL *shakes her head,* OLIVE *continues delightedly*) Reuben—wouldn't it kill yer? Reuben!

PEARL. It's out the Bible.

OLIVE. Is it? I didn't know that. (*There is the sound of a car horn offstage.* OLIVE *reacts excitedly and swoops to window*) Oooh, me beads . . . that's not them, is it? No. Car up the road. Nearly died. (*Surveying table*) Not that there's much more to do. I'll get some glasses out 'n' bring the salad in. (*She exits, a second or two later breaking into a faulty soprano offstage, taking up the melody from the radio.* PEARL *stares room over, then crosses to close French windows. She moves to pick up photograph, and studies it closely.* OLIVE *re-enters, carrying glasses. The daylight is gradually fading from the room*) Hey, did you hear that Charlie in the saloon bar last night? All the time we was cleanin' up he kept whistlin' "Old Black Magic." (*Placing glasses*) Havin' a go at me, a course; he's known about Roo for years, and he always gets in a crack every time. Not that I ever let on, mind yer. (*She looks across at* PEARL, *who is frowning over the photograph, and says with a note of reserve*) Well, what's the matter now?

PEARL. Nothin'. I'm just havin' another look.

OLIVE (*Moving in and taking photograph from her*) If you don't watch out, you're gunna start hatin' the poor bloke before he even gets here.
(*She goes back to the sideboard with it.*)

PEARL. No, I won't. (*Sitting, righteously*) At the same time, I'm not lettin' myself in for any nasty mess, either.

OLIVE (*Contemptuously*). Nasty mess! What makes you think I'd be havin' anythin' to do with it if there was any mess about it?

PEARL. It doesn't matter for you, you haven't got a daughter to think of. Vera's just at that age I gotta be careful. If she cottons on to me doin' anythin' wrong, she's likely to break out the same way.

OLIVE (*In quick hostility, snapping off radio*). Now look, that's one thing I'm not gunna stand for. Right from the start!

PEARL. What?

OLIVE. You know what! That respectable mother stunt. Don't you try and put that over on me.

PEARL. I didn't say a word.

OLIVE. You said wrong, didn't yer? 'N' nasty mess? That's enough. I've told you over 'n' over again what this lay-off is, yet every time you open your mouth you make it sound like somethin'—low and dirty. Well, if that's the way you look at it, you don't have to stay, y'know—nobody's forcin' you to make any decisions about it—you can get your bags from the hall and clear out before they get here.

PEARL (*Defensively*).   Just because I don't think it's altogether proper.

OLIVE.   Yeh. Just because of that.

PEARL.   Nobody would say it was a decent way of livin'.

OLIVE.   Wouldn't they? I would! I've knocked about with all sorts from the time I was fourteen, and I've never come across anythin' more decent in my life. Decency is—it depends on the people. And don't you say it doesn't!

PEARL.   I meant decent like marriage. That's different, you said yourself it was.

OLIVE (*With a slight shudder*).   It's different all right. Compared to all the marriages I know, what I got is—(*She gropes for depth of expression*) is five months of heaven every year. And it's the same for them. Seven months they spend up there killin' themselves in the cane season, and then they come down here to live a little. That's what the lay-off is. Not just playin' around and spendin' a lot of money, but a time for livin'. You think I haven't sized that up against what other women have? I laugh at them every time they try to tell me. Even waitin' for Roo to come back is more excitin' than anythin' they've got. So you make up your mind right now— you're either gunna be polite to them and hang on until you get to know Barney well enough to decide, or you're gunna get out of here right now.

(OLIVE *crosses to table and wrenches top from bottle of*

15

beer, while PEARL *fiddles uneasily. There is a pause. Finally* PEARL *breaks the silence, speaking with a rather helpless shrug.*)

PEARL. Well, I dunno what it's gunna be like livin' here if you can't even pass an opinion on things. (OLIVE *gives vent to a loud "Aah" of derision and pours two glasses of beer.* PEARL *continues, more defensively than ever*) That's all I was doin', passin' an opinion. Anyone's entitled to do that.
(*Holding the two glasses,* OLIVE *thrusts one at her.*)

OLIVE. Here, sit down and shut up if you can't talk sense.
(OLIVE *moves to window, and leans against piano, looking out through lace curtains and sipping her beer.* PEARL *speaks, rather indignantly.*)

PEARL. You told me yourself they hardly ever write you from the time they go away till the time they come back.

OLIVE (*Without turning*). They don't have to write me, I know where they are. Workin' their way through up north.

PEARL. Yes, but at least they could let you know how they're gettin' on.

OLIVE (*Slightly exasperated*). What—cuttin' sugar cane? What can they say about that? Roo's one of the best men they've got—runs his own gang—but even down here you never get him yappin' about his season's tally. That's all his part of it.

PEARL (*Defeated*). Well, it beats me how you can stand it. I know with Wallie I used to worry all the time. Even if he was late comin' home from work, I used to worry.

16

OLIVE. With these you don't have to. These are men—not the sort we see go rollin' home to their wives every night, but men.

PEARL. I know, you keep tellin' me. I never knew there was any difference.

OLIVE. You never knew! (*There is a pause, and then she speaks in a voice of defiant pride*) Nancy used to say it was how they'd walk into the pub as if they owned it—even just in the way they walked you could spot it. All round would be the regulars—soft city blokes havin' their drinks and their little arguments, and then in would come Roo and Barney. They wouldn't say anythin'—they didn't have to—there'd just be the two of them walkin' in, then a kind of wait for a second or two, and quiet. After that, without a word, the regulars'd stand aside to let 'em through, just as if they was a—a coupla kings. She always reckoned they made the rest of the mob look like a bunch of skinned rabbits. (*Softly*) Poor old Nancy.

PEARL. She got what she wanted, didn't she?

OLIVE (*Hungrily*). I'd like to ask her. Right now, with them expected any minute, and her sittin' chained up to that—book bloke—I'd like to ask her if she thinks it was worth it. And I bet that'd be one question she wouldn't be able to laugh her way out of!

PEARL (*After a pause, unconvincingly*). Well, you know her, I don't. I'm sorry if I put you out.

OLIVE (*Mollified, as she goes to turn on standard lamp above piano*). Ah—my fault for flyin' off the handle. It was just that for a moment you sounded like my mother. She's fond of

Roo, y'know, but every time he's away and we have a row, Emma throws him up at me like a dirty dishcloth. Every time!

PEARL (*Sympathetically*). I know. Aunt of mine was like that. Used to store everythin' up and let it go at family funerals.

OLIVE (*Warmly*). Oh, chronic! Doesn't it make you mad? (*She crosses and switches on second lamp.*)

PEARL. They just want to make trouble, really.

OLIVE. That's all. Here, empty that and let's have another. (*She downs her drink.*)

PEARL. No, you have one, I haven't started this yet. Feel a bit gassy.

OLIVE (*Pouring her own*). C'mon, we'll have to get rid of this bottle, otherwise they're gunna think we started off without them.

PEARL (*Interrupting*). Listen. . . .

OLIVE. What? (*She pauses, then rushes to the window as a car horn sounds offstage in mid-distance*) Too late—that's them now!
(*She sweeps into action, gulps down most of her beer, grabs the bottle and rushes over to stow it and the glass under the table.* PEARL *rises and gestures with her glass, in a near panic.*)

PEARL. What'll I do with this?

OLIVE. Drink it, of course. (*She dashes over to pick up small paper bag from sideboard, transfers something from it to her mouth, then thrusts the bag on* PEARL, *who is hastily swallowing beer and tidying her hair at the mantelpiece)* Peppermints!

> *(Meanwhile, offstage, the taxi has drawn up in front of the house and has sounded a merry "Om diddly om pom" on the horn. As* OLIVE *moves toward front door we hear excited voices.)*

ROO. Hey, wake up in there.

BARNEY. You little trimmer, Emma, you little beauty—(BARNEY *moves easily up onto the veranda, carrying* EMMA *over his shoulder,* EMMA *shrieking with laughter and pretended anger, beating at him with aged fists. As* OLIVE *opens the door,* BARNEY *yells)* Hey, missus, where's your rubbish heap? Got some old sugar gone dry. (*Laughing,* OLIVE *stands aside, and they rock into the house, coming into prominence in the arch entrance.* ROO *enters onto front veranda,* OLIVE *moves into his arms, and they kiss long and warmly.* PEARL *is regarding* BARNEY's *antics with* EMMA *in a restrained apprehension which she hopes looks like amusement, when* BARNEY *focuses on her for the first time. Slapping* EMMA's *rear and letting her slide down onto sofa)* Here, here, stop all this, you wicked old thing, you oughta have more sense, playin' up like that in front of visitors.

EMMA (*Pummeling him*). It was you—you started it—

BARNEY (*Holding her off, his eyes on* PEARL). That's enough, cut it out now or I really will toss you out with the rubbish—look at the lady watchin' you!

EMMA (*Screwing round*). Oh—her! She's the one I was tellin' you about.

BARNEY. Is she? Well, you nip out and give 'em a hand with the bags then. (*He puts her to one side and moves down on* PEARL, *but* EMMA *stands her ground. She is a wizened, life-battered wisp of a woman, nearly seventy, with no illusions about humanity, expecting the worst from it, and generally crowing with cynical delight when her expectations are fulfilled. Her eye, as she watches this meeting, is definitely satirical.* BARNEY *swaggers down, and* PEARL *stands in front of fireplace, self-consciously formal. He pauses before her, with a wide boyish grin*) 'Lo. S'pose they've told you about me, have they? I'm Barney.

PEARL (*Stammering*). Yes, Olive did mention—I'm Missus Cunningham. How d'yer do.

(*She offers her hand awkwardly and he takes it, not shaking it, but holding it gently, as if to feel its weight.*)

BARNEY. I'm pretty good. How's yerself?

(*He puts his other hand on top of hers, and, still grinning broadly, forces her to meet his eyes.* BARNEY *owes most of his success in love to this natural technique; he has an overwhelming weakness for women, and makes them recognize it. Previous mention of him as a little man is not quite correct. He is short, certainly, but not much below medium height, and solidly built. Probably his constant association with the bigger* ROO *emphasizes his lack of inches. His manner is assertive, confident and impudently bright, perhaps a little overdone as a defiance to his forty years and the beginning of a pot belly.* PEARL *tries to carry off her embarrassment lightly.*)

PEARL. Oh, y'know—a bit hot.

(EMMA *gives a cackle of laughter and skitters off toward kitchen, passing* OLIVE, *who, after her close silent meeting on the veranda with* ROO, *is returning to the front room. Meanwhile* ROO *has gone offstage and shortly reappears with two suitcases.*)

BARNEY (*Calling after* EMMA). Cut out the rough stuff now.

OLIVE (*Embracing* BARNEY). What's the matter with the old girl?

BARNEY (*Giggling*). Phenyl decay, I think. It's getting her down.

OLIVE (*Moving into room*). I suppose you two have met by now—uh?

BARNEY. Well, we've got as far as Barney and Missus Cunningham.

OLIVE. Ah, Pearl it is. Don't let's have any of that Mister and Missus stuff. Pearl!

BARNEY. Pearl! (*He smiles, then swings jovially up to* OLIVE) And how about you? Not down at Swanston Street to see us in.

(*He slaps his hands together suggestively, and she fends him off.*)

OLIVE. Cut it out now—didn't want to have you two meetin' at the Airways 'mong a lot of people, that's all.

BARNEY. What—was you frightened I'd go off like a jet or somethin'?

(*He turns and winks at* PEARL, *who smiles feebly in return.*)

OLIVE. We'd have brought you down pretty quick if you had! Where's Roo? Come on, Roo . . . (ROO *detaches himself from the arch against which he has been leaning, and* OLIVE *goes up to take him lovingly by the arm, and steers him down*) I want you to meet a friend of mine. Pearl Cunningham—Roo Webber.

PEARL (*Shaking hands*). How d'yer do.

ROO. Pleased to meet yer. (ROO *smiles slowly at her, and* PEARL *relaxes a little. He is a man's man with a streak of gentleness, a mixture that invites confidence. Tall, thirty-eight years of age, fair hair tinged with gray, a rather battered face with a well-cut mouth. Recent experiences have etched a faint line of bewilderment between his eyes, a sign of the first serious mental struggle he has ever had in his life, but his manner seems free and easygoing. Both men are deeply tanned, a strong contrast to the white fleshiness of the women*) Missus Cunningham, is it?

OLIVE (*Quickly*). Yes, she's a widow.

ROO (*Understandingly*). Ah.
    (BARNEY *sees walking sticks on mantelpiece and grabs one in a sudden burst of high spirits.*)

BARNEY. Hey, look at this, willya? Where is she? Where's that Bubba?

OLIVE. Home—

BARNEY (*Heading for windows*). What's she doin' at home? She oughta be in here—
    (*He pulls open windows and steps onto back veranda.*)

OLIVE. She's comin' in after—
(OLIVE *makes to arrest* BARNEY, *but* ROO *holds her.*)

BARNEY (*Cupping his hands and yelling*). Buubbaa—what are yer hidin' for? Reckon we're gunna lam into you with a walkin' stick or somethin'?
(BUBBA's *voice, distant and full of laughter, answers from offstage.*)

BUBBA. Take a bigger man than you, Mister Ibbot.
(ROO *joins* BARNEY *on veranda as* OLIVE *guides* PEARL *soothingly to sofa.*)

OLIVE. Don't worry, they'll calm down in a min-⎫
  ute—   ⎪
ROO (*Yelling to* BUBBA). What about me, then? ⎬ *Together*
  (BUBBA *laughs in distance*) How're you goin', ⎪
  Bub?   ⎭

BUBBA. Fine.

OLIVE (*Coming to French window*). Hey, cut it out, you two, it's Sunday. Come inside, you'll see her after.
(OLIVE *takes* BARNEY's *arm to draw him into room.*)

ROO (*Calling in farewell*). Don't you be too long comin' in, now.

BUBBA. I won't.
(*Inside room,* BARNEY *sweeps* OLIVE *off her feet, twirls her around, cuddles his cheek next to hers and speaks expressively.*)

BARNEY. Ah, my favorite barmaid.

OLIVE. You'd better not let Pearl hear you say that.

BARNEY (*Delightedly*). Don't tell me she's . . .

OLIVE (*Nodding*). Same pub—same bar!

BARNEY (*Jubilantly moving in to sit by* PEARL *on sofa*) Whacko! That makes it just like old times.

(PEARL *wriggles uneasily,* EMMA *rushes into room, furious.*)

EMMA. Thieves—dirty thieves! Pinchin' an old woman's food while her back's turned—

BARNEY. Hullo—what's bitin' Emma?

EMMA. Vinegar, that's what's bitin' me. Who's been at my vinegar?

OLIVE. I took a tiny little skerrick to put in a salad—

EMMA (*Fiercely*). A whole half-bottle, that's how much a skerrick it was. Robbin' your own mother. Whose house do you think this is, anyway?

OLIVE. I pay the rates and taxes—

EMMA. Never mind that, I own it, and things in it is private. I've told you before to keep away from my cupboard.

OLIVE. That makes us quits then. I told you to keep away from the Airways.

EMMA. The community singin' was out early, else I wouldn't 'ave gone near the place. And you oughta be damned glad I did go, or these larrikins wouldn't be here. . . .

BARNEY (*Covering up*). Hold your horses, Emma, you dunno what you're talkin' about.

EMMA. Don't I just?

ROO. Kickin' up a fuss about a bit of vinegar. You got enough to buy a new bottle, didn't yer?

EMMA (*Scornfully*). Two quid—two lousy fiddlies—a fortune! (*To her daughter*) I'm drummin' you for the last time, you touch my cupboard again and I'm off down to Russell Street.

. . .

(BARNEY, ROO *and* OLIVE *join in a chorus; it is evidently a well-known threat.*)

BARNEY.
OLIVE. } Just as fast as me legs can carry me!
ROO.

EMMA (*Terribly*). Yez'll be laughin' the other side your face once the johns git after yer!
(*She stumps out.* BARNEY *calls after her.*)

BARNEY. What do you need vinegar for anyway, you wicked old thing, you're sour enough now.
(*There is a general laugh.* EMMA's *entrance has dissipated a lot of strangeness.*)

ROO. Better get the bags out of the way, I s'pose.
(*He moves toward arch,* OLIVE *interposes quickly.*)

OLIVE. Just your own, then. Don't take Barney's up—

BARNEY. Why? What's the matter with mine?

OLIVE. You're big and ugly enough to carry 'em yourself.
(ROO *laughs shortly, picks up one of the cases and exits upstairs.* BARNEY *meanwhile threatens* OLIVE *playfully.*)

BARNEY. Oh, I can see I'm gunna have to take you in hand, they been lettin' yer run wild—

OLIVE. Yeh, stout and oysters. (*She moves to mantelpiece*) Here, I've got a telegram for you. Came yesterday.

BARNEY (*Taking it*). For me? (*Eyeing it off*) Wonder what's wrong?

OLIVE. It'll be inside. (*He begins to open it reluctantly.* OLIVE *crosses to* PEARL, *and speaks with a broad hint in her voice*) Pearl, go out and rescue that salad from the old girl, will you? She's just as likely to tip it down the gully trap.

PEARL (*Thankfully*). Yes. She might, too.
(PEARL *exits discreetly.* BARNEY *reading the telegram, gives an "Ah" of fond relief.*)

BARNEY. Whaddya know—it's from Nancy.

OLIVE (*Tightly*). I guessed it would be.

BARNEY (*Reading*). Up there Cazaly, lots of love—Nance. (*Folding slip*) Where's she livin' now?

OLIVE. Never you mind, you leave her alone.

BARNEY. Just wanted to say hello.

OLIVE. Yes, we all know your sort of hello. You had your chance with Nancy.

26

BARNEY. What'd you bet I couldn't get her back?

OLIVE. It wouldn't do you a scrap of good. Not in this place, anyway. The day she got married I swore I'd never have the two of you here together again no matter what happened. Pearl's the one you've got to concentrate on.
(BARNEY *turns away easily.*)

BARNEY. Ah, Pearl'll be all right.

OLIVE. Will she? Don't you be too sure of that. 'Fact, she's got her bags piled up by the stairs, 'n' if she doesn't take to you by tomorrow mornin' she's shiftin' out.

BARNEY. Why? What's the matter?

OLIVE. She's not too shook on the whole thing. Doesn't understand it, for one thing; then she's got a daughter, kid of eighteen. Livin' with relations at present, but it makes Pearl nervous, she's scared of puttin' her foot wrong. Then when I wised her up about your handful of errors, that made her more nervous still—

BARNEY (*Astounded*). Don't tell me she's jibbin', at her age . . . ?

OLIVE. Oh, it's not for herself. She just doesn't think you've done the right thing.

BARNEY (*Indignantly*). What the hell does she know about it? Did you tell her how regular I've been, coughin' up every week?

OLIVE. Yes, but she sez it's not the money, it's the principle.

BARNEY (*Disgustedly*). Oh—one of them, is she?

27

OLIVE. No, she ain't, she's a very decent sort. 'Matter of fact, I think she's got some idea of reformin' you.

BARNEY. Yes? Well, that's been tried before today, too.

OLIVE. She's got this kid, Vera, and I'd say she was lookin' for some sort of nest for the pair of 'em.

BARNEY. With me? (*She nods*) Well, what a thing to let a bloke in for!

OLIVE. You don't have to do anythin' about it if you don't want to—not even talk to her. But I'm warnin' you, you pass her up for any of those painted crows of yours, don't think you can bring 'em home here to live.

BARNEY. Looks like Pearl or nothin' then, eh? (*Expansively*) Righto, I'll have a word with her after. She'll be jake.

OLIVE. Pretty sure of yourself, aren't yer.

BARNEY (*Winking*). My oath.

OLIVE. Don't kid yourself, Barney. It won't be any walkover.

BARNEY. No? Well, now I'll tell you somethin'. You've got a bit of a battle ahead of you, too. (*She looks questioningly at him. He speaks on a quieter note*) You heard what Emma said—'bout if it hadn't been for her we wouldn't be here? 'S true.

OLIVE (*Disbelievingly*). Aah. . . .

BARNEY. I'm tellin' yer—when you weren't down at the terminal, for a minute or two Roo was talkin' about tryin' to get in some joint he knows at North Melbourne—

OLIVE (*Staring*). Lots of times I haven't been down to meet yez. Saturdays . . .

BARNEY. He wasn't mad at yer not bein' there. It's nothin' like that.

OLIVE. What then?

BARNEY (*Hesitatingly*). He's broke.

OLIVE. Roo?

BARNEY. I had to buy his ticket down.

OLIVE (*Incredulously*). But how can he be broke? Before he even gets here?

BARNEY (*Sighing*). You dunno what a bloody awful season it's been, everythin' went wrong. Worst we've ever had, I reckon.

OLIVE. Couldn't you get work?

BARNEY (*Scornfully*). Oh it wasn't that, the work was there, any amount of it. It was just plain bad luck. (*She makes a move toward arch*) Now don't go runnin' up to him, he's chockablock, you'd better hear it from me.
(*She hesitates, then returns.*)

OLIVE (*Flatly*). What happened?

BARNEY. Well, first set off, Roo, the silly cow, strains his back — There's no need to throw a fit, nothin' serious, nearly better. But it slowed him down all through the season, see. (*Frankly, putting cards on the table*) Roo's a pretty hard man, y'know, on the job. Got no use for anyone can't pull their weight; and bein' able to pick and choose almost, 'coz every-

29

one knows he's one of the best gangers there is, gen'rally he gets a champion bunch together. But he's gotta be hard doin' it sometimes. (*Facing her*) This year he got the boys to turn off Tony Moreno. You must've heard us talk of Tony, real character, everyone likes him, but anyway Roo thought he was gettin' too slow. Instead he takes on a big young bloke we'd heard a lot about, name of Johnnie Dowd. Cracked up to be as fast as lightnin'.

OLIVE. Was he?

BARNEY. Yeh. Not as good as Roo, when he's fit, mind yer, but he could run rings round the best of us. And this time he even made Roo look a bit sick.

OLIVE. Did Roo know?

BARNEY. Well, that's the point. He's fast at both loadin' and cuttin', this Dowdie, just the same as Roo, and it's not often you get fellers like that. The boys noticed it and they started pickin', tellin' Roo he'd have to watch out or they'd have a new ganger. Didn't mean nothin' by it, just jokin', but Roo takes it up the wrong way. Instead of pointin' out that he had a bad back, he puts himself to work by this Dowd—gunna show him up, see. Well, that's just what he shouldna done, the kid toweled him up proper. I never seen Roo git so mad, in no time at all he'd made it a runnin' fight between 'em. . . .

OLIVE. The damned fool!

BARNEY. That's what I told him. Calm down, I sez, what's it matter. . . .

OLIVE (*Exasperated*). And with a busted back—how the hell could he win?

BARNEY (*Shrugging*). I dunno. Reckons he's twice as good as everyone else, I s'pose. Anyway, 'bout two months ago, flamin' hot day it was, gettin' near knock-off time, they had a blue.

OLIVE. Bad?

BARNEY. Pretty bad. I was right on the spot when it happened. Started off over nothin'. They was workin' side by side, and when Dowdie finishes the strip he looks back to see how far behind Roo was. Well, right at that moment Roo's knees went. Never seen anythin' like it, they just buckled under him and there he was, down on the ground. This strikes Dowd as bein' funny, see, and he starts to laugh. Well, that did it. Roo went him and it was on, cane knives and the lot. Took six of us to separate 'em; could've been murder, I reckon. 'Course the boys all blamed Roo for it, so he did his block again, packed up his gear and walked off. (*There is an uncomfortable pause*) I didn't see him after that till I picked him up in Brisbane a week ago.

OLIVE. You didn't go with him?

BARNEY. No.

OLIVE. Why not?

BARNEY (*Disturbed*). I dunno. It was all messed up. You know what Roo's always been to me, a sort of little tin god. I've never seen him in the wrong before.

OLIVE. He's been wrong plenty of times.

BARNEY (*Strongly*). Not to me, he hasn't. This was the first time.

OLIVE.   Well, go on. What happened?

BARNEY.   Nothin'. He went off and I stayed. Then, like I said, I picked him up in Brisbane a week ago. By then he hardly had a razoo.

OLIVE.   What was it—booze?

BARNEY.   Yeh. Been hittin' it pretty heavy. We didn't talk much about it, I think he's got a spite on me for not walkin' out with him. But honest, the way I felt at the time, I just couldn't— (*She is staring accusingly at him, and he escapes her eyes with a twisted shrug*) Apart from that, I needed the money. And a course I had to put me foot in it all over again by tellin' him how they made Dowdie ganger in his place, and what a bottlin' job he done. (*Unperceived by either of them,* ROO *moves downstairs to stand in entrance*) Well, you gotta give him credit, for a kid he made a very smart fist of it. . . .

ROO (*Crudely*).   Yeh. And have you told her 'bout the big booze-up he threw when yez all got back to Cairns?
    (BARNEY *looks at him and then turns away, ashamed.*)

BARNEY.   Bein' sarcastic won't get you anywhere.

ROO.   Blabber-gutsin' doesn't take you far, either.

OLIVE.   It's not his fault, I asked him. (*Addressing* BARNEY) Better take your cases up. (*He moves toward arch and she remembers, adding hastily*) Oh, you're in the little back room for tonight.
    (BARNEY *grins wryly, with a flash of his former spirits.*)

BARNEY.   Is it as bad as that?
    (*She nods, and he carries on to pick up his bag and exits upstairs. There is an embarrassed pause.*)

ROO. If I know him when he opens his big trap, I don't s'pose he's left me much to tell.

OLIVE *(On edge)*. One or two things. Where you was thinkin' of going to in North Melbourne, for instance?

ROO *(Shrugging irritably)*. Aah, who the hell cares about that?

OLIVE. Me, for one. I'd like to know what's around there you can't get here.

ROO *(Sulkily)*. I got a kind of cousin, used to keep a grocery shop. Bloke named Wallace.

OLIVE. Well, that's lovely, that is. After seventeen years, the first time there's trouble, that's who you go to—bloke named Wallace in a grocery shop.

ROO *(Turning on her angrily)*. Olive, I'm broke. D'yer understand? Flat, stony, stinkin' broke!

OLIVE *(Shrilly)*. Yeh, and I'd care a lot for that, wouldn't I? That's how I've always met you, standin' on the front veranda with a cash register, lookin' like a—like a bloody—
    (She breaks off, overcome by sudden gasping tears, gropes for a handkerchief. ROO is troubled and comes from behind to take her in his arms, drawing her to him with the gentle ease of long familiarity.)

ROO *(Humbly)*. Olive, I wasn't thinkin'. Aw, c'mon, hon, you know I didn't mean that.

OLIVE *(Muffled)*. Fellers like you—yer ought to be kicked.

ROO. I was lookin' for somethin' to make it easy.

OLIVE (*Twisting in his arms to face him*). What's wrong with me? I'm workin', ain't I?

ROO (*Stubbornly*). I won't bludge on you.

OLIVE (*Tearfully*). You can lay off here just as you always have, and—and I can—

ROO (*Finally*). I won't bludge. I'll get a job or somethin'.

OLIVE. A job?

ROO. Well, somethin' or other, we'll think about it tomorrow. Now stop your cryin' and let's forget it. It'll work out all right. You pleased to see me?

OLIVE (*Hoarsely*). If you hadna come I would have gone lookin' for you with a razor.
(*They hold each other in a long kiss.*)

ROO. You know what we both need, don't yer? A nice long beer to cool us down. . . .
(OLIVE *draws away from him, giggling, her spirits already swinging back on the upsurge.*)

OLIVE. I've already had some. Me and Pearl was in the middle of crackin' a bottle when you got here. (*She fishes it out from under the table and holds it aloft*) Look, we hid it so you wouldn't know.

ROO. Well, what a pair of tomtits you are! (*Suddenly it seems very funny, and they roar with laughter. She rushes up to arch, he crosses to sideboard, turns on the radio, which presently plays gay infectious music*) C'mon, my tongue's hangin' out after that long plane trip.

OLIVE (*Calling up stairs*). Up there, Cazaly—come on down—
the party's on—

ROO. Get 'em all in . . .

OLIVE (*Calling toward kitchen*). Pearl, don't be all night with
that salad. I told him . . .

PEARL (*Off*). Be right with you.
> (BARNEY *comes downstairs with an armful of presents,
> among them the seventeenth doll. He sneaks past* OLIVE
> *to enter room and hand doll to* ROO, *who quickly hides it
> behind his back. Meanwhile,* OLIVE *calls to* EMMA.)

OLIVE. Come on, Emma, Roo's poured you a beer.
> (EMMA's *voice is heard off, raised in mechanical fury.*)

EMMA. Wouldn't soil me lips.
> (*Laughing,* OLIVE *comes back from the kitchen entrance.*
> PEARL *enters bearing a large bowl of salad, followed by*
> EMMA. *When* OLIVE *is at archway* ROO *holds high the gift.*)

ROO. Here you are—the seventeenth doll!
> (OLIVE *gives a cry of sheer happiness and rushes down
> into his encircling arms.* BARNEY *is standing by, watching
> with a grin. Music reaches a peak.*)

Curtain

Scene Two

Time: The following morning.

The room has a stale, used look, the remnants of last night's meal still clutter the table, empty glasses and bottles are scattered about. A corner of the tablecloth hangs down as though some-one has dragged on it. Wrapping paper clutters the floor.

The curtain rises on an empty stage, then EMMA *enters from the kitchen with a floor rug which she takes onto the front ve-randa and hangs over the wrought-iron rail. She looks at the weather and sniffs the air. After a minute she returns to the front door, calling.*

EMMA. Better take your coat with you, Olly, it looks like rain.

OLIVE (*Off*). A day like today—you're mad.

EMMA. All right then, don't be told. (*She exits into front gar-den, muttering. Returns with two milk bottles and a news-paper. In the hallway she meets* ROO, *who has descended stairs. He is a little morning-after, but not much. She thrusts the newspaper at him*) Here—there's gunna be a cool change.

ROO. Them weather blokes don't know nothin'.

EMMA. It ain't the weather blokes says so, it's me.

ROO (*Grinning*). Ah. That's different.

(EMMA *snorts and exits to kitchen.* ROO *throws paper onto table, decides that the room can do with some fresh air. He opens French windows and steps out onto back ve-*

36

randa, where he stands yawning in the morning sunlight and scratching his belly. After a moment something attracts his attention and he moves out of sight. There is the clink of beer bottles being collected, and he re-enters, carrying four empties. OLIVE *enters from kitchen, dressed for work in a light summer frock. She is finishing off a slice of toast.*)

OLIVE. Roo?

ROO. That silly Barney, throwing these out on the veranda. Kid's trick. He oughta stop doing that.
(*He puts bottles to one side.*)

OLIVE. Pearl didn't like it either.

ROO (*Sitting and picking up newspaper*). I don't reckon he's gunna hit it off with her.

OLIVE. Neither do I. Not by the way she's talkin'. Yer should've heard what she said about him tryin' her door last night

ROO (*Opening paper*). Well, she could've expected that.

OLIVE. 'S what I told her. (*Rubbing the back of her hand against his bristly cheek*) If you'd stayed in bed a bit longer, I would have brought your breakfast up.

ROO (*Stolidly reading*). You know I don't like eatin' in bed.

OLIVE. Just for a change. (*Begins to massage his shoulder*) How's your back? (ROO *glances up at her*) Barney told me how you strained it—least, he didn't say how you did it, just about how it slowed you down so much.

ROO. Trust Barney.

OLIVE. How did you do it?

ROO (*Grimly*). Ask him, he's got all the news.
(*He returns to his reading.*)

OLIVE (*Playfully*). All right, no one's gunna make an invalid
of you, I know you hate bein' sick. (*She moves away to pick
up the seventeenth doll from rocking chair, and stands strok-
ing it tenderly*) Prettier than ever—You know, I think they
take more trouble with them than they used to. There's more
tinsel and—and they're dressed better.

ROO. They're just the same as they always was.

OLIVE (*Protectively*). No, they're not. Someone's takin' special
care. Other times they've been pretty, but this one's beautiful.
You can see. (*She holds the doll almost as if it were a baby,
and says suddenly*) You know why I like the dolls more than
anythin' else you've brought down? (*He shakes his head*)
Well, the birds and coral and—and butterflies and stuff—all
that you got me 'coz I wanted to know what it was like up
there. But the dolls—they're somethin' you thought of by
yourself. So they're special! (*He grunts, embarrassed. She
fluffs out doll's skirts*) And don't make noises at me, they are.
Where'll I put her?

ROO (*Glancing around*). Gettin' a bit crowded, maybe you
should start upstairs.

OLIVE (*Crossing to vase*). No, I won't, she's stayin' right here
with the others. (*Places doll in vase*) Look at her now, she
just dazzles yer.

ROO (*Touched, but gruffly*). She's all right.

38

OLIVE. Beautiful. (*She moves to him to kiss the side of his head and run her fingers through his hair*) Beautiful. What do you reckon you'll do today?

ROO (*Absently*). Oh. I'll find something.
(*He turns pages.*)

OLIVE. Do you think you might drop in at the pub?

ROO. Might.

OLIVE (*Gripping his hair and tugging gently*). Well, don't put yourself out, will you? I was thinkin' I might get you to book me a few seats. There's some good shows on I've been holdin' off on. . . .
(EMMA *appears in arch carrying an empty tray which she places on sideboard.*)

EMMA (*Resentfully*). Anybody wants breakfast better come and get it, I'm not gunna keep it hot all day.

OLIVE. Did you give Barney a yell?

EMMA. I'm not yellin' for anyone, I got enough to do. (*She comes into room, clicking her tongue*) And just look at this, will yer? 'Course it doesn't matter to you, all youse have to do is make a pigsty of the joint and then go off and loll around bars all day.

OLIVE. Strikes me you did your fair share of the damage. And if you don't want to touch it, you don't have to, I'll do it tonight.

EMMA. Yeh, I'll bet you will.
(OLIVE *speaks to* ROO, *who is still immersed in the paper.*)

OLIVE. Will you get the tickets, then?

ROO (*Looking up*). Let's leave it for a coupla days, eh? I got to settle a few other things first.

OLIVE (*Restrainedly*). Righto. But you have to book ahead, y'know, if you want decent seats.
(*She leaves the room, and a moment later is heard calling up the stairs, "Barney—breakfast." ROO returns to his paper, EMMA tidies the room.*)

EMMA (*Slyly*). Was that why you only gave me a quid at the Airways?

ROO. Why?

EMMA. 'Coz you're broke.

ROO. Who sez I'm broke?

EMMA. Heard you yellin' it out yesterday—flat, stony, stinkin' broke, y'said.

ROO. Nothin' wrong with your hearin', is there.

EMMA. I 'ave to keep me ears open in this house. Learn enough to pertect myself. Gotta bit of a cheek, haven't yer, turnin' up like that?

ROO (*Equally*). Lay off, Emma. I'll make it up to you.

EMMA. Yeh, I've heard that before, too.

ROO. This place—(*Reading*) Lyman Paint Company, Weston Street—is that anywhere near here?

EMMA. Around the corner, 'bout three blocks down.

ROO (*A grunt of satisfaction*). Ah.

EMMA. That Barney—is 'e broke too?

ROO. Don't reckon so. He oughta have pretty near his usual packet.

EMMA. Just as well. I wouldn't think of helpin' him out.

ROO (*Twinkling*). Was you thinkin' of helpin' me?

EMMA. I might. (*Hastily*) Only a loan, mind yer. I'd want it back again.

ROO. How much—a fiver?

EMMA (*Coolly*). Smart Alec, ain't yer? What d'yer say to fifty?

ROO. Quid? (*She nods*) You got fifty quid?

EMMA (*Triumphantly*). I got more, I got nearly—well, never mind. And don't you let on to anyone I even got fifty. But that's what I could let you have, if you want it.

ROO (*Admiringly*). You beaut! Who'd you pinch it from—Olive?

EMMA. Her? What I git from her hardly pays for me community. No, I got me own ways of earnin' a few bob.

ROO. I'll bet you have. Keepin' nit for the S.P. bookies, eh—drummin' up trade for the sly grogs—

(BUBBA, *dressed for the street, enters on side veranda.*)

EMMA. Ask no questions, you get told no lies. (*She catches sight of* BUBBA *standing at window*) Well, you're an early bird—don't tell me you've come to help me clean up?

41

BUBBA (*Shaking her head*). I'm off to work, I only dropped in for a minute. . . .

EMMA. Thought it was too good to be true. Same as usual—everythin' left to the old girl.
(*She exits to kitchen with tray.* ROO *grins at* BUBBA.)

ROO. She never misses a trick, does she? Come on in, Bub—how are yer? Didn't get much of a chance to talk to you last night.

BUBBA. No, I—I didn't stay long. (*Breathlessly*) Look, I've got somethin' for Barney.

ROO. He's not up yet.

BUBBA (*Holding out envelope*). Will you give 'em to him, then? I don't want Olive to see them—they're some snaps I took of Nancy's weddin'.

ROO (*Accepting envelope*). Oh. (*With a touch of reserve*) What was it like?

BUBBA. All right. Not big, y'know, just people *he* knew; I think I was the only one Nance invited. But she looked very pretty, a deep sort of blue it was. I thought Barney'd like to have the photos.

ROO. Yeh. Did you cry?

BUBBA (*Nodding*). So did she.

ROO. I'll tell you somethin'. I think Barney did, too. He went away on his own a whole afternoon—somethin' I've never seen him do before. Whenever he's been in trouble he's always wanted someone standin' by holdin' his hand. This time he didn't even want me near him.

BUBBA.   I knew he'd feel like that. I told Olive. Roo, why didn't he come down? Four letters we wrote him—

ROO.   Well, first I think he didn't believe she'd do it. Then, when it looked certain, he couldn't make the effort. He's been dodgin' it a long time, you know.

BUBBA.   It's awful to think of the two of them, feelin' like they do, and yet messin' it up like that.

ROO (*Trying to lift the conversation from potential embarrassment*).   Yeh. But what about you? I s'pose the next thing we know you'll be poppin' off, too.

BUBBA.   No. I don't think so.

ROO (*Rolling a cigarette*).   What about that Mac feller was chasin' you round when we left?

BUBBA.   Who? Oh—Douggie! Haven't seen him since June or July somethin'. I been out with half a dozen since then.

ROO (*Teasing*).   Strikes me you're gunna grow up to be your Uncle Barney all over again.

BUBBA (*Quietly*).   I'm twenty-two now. How much more d'you reckon I have to grow!

ROO.   Ah, c'mon, I was only kiddin'. We all know you've left school.

BUBBA.   Yes. (*She hesitates, spurring herself to ask the question*) Roo, can I ask you somethin'?

ROO. What?

BUBBA. About the lay-off . . .

ROO. What about it?

BUBBA. It's goin' to be just the same, isn't it? I mean, it's still goin' to be Selby at Christmas time, and . . . and all the rest. You won't alter anythin'?

ROO. 'Course we won't, you little dill. Why should we?

BUBBA (*Smiling tremulously*). I was scared—with Nancy gone—

ROO. The rest of us are still here, ain't we? What the hell, 'course it'll be the same.
   (*She rushes over to hug him impulsively, as* EMMA *enters with a bowl of fruit.*)

EMMA (*Dryly*). Only droppin' in for a minute, you said. Any more of this and I don't reckon Woolworth's'll be openin' up today at all.

BUBBA. As if they'd miss me. (*Moving to window*) Come in and see us if you've got the time, Roo. I'm on the perfumes.

ROO. Yeh. That's just about my form, ain't it?
   (BUBBA *laughs and exits.* EMMA *places fruit on table.*)

EMMA. You'd be in to see her soon enough if she was servin' beer, I bet. (*Sternly*) What about that money—do you want it, or don't yer?

ROO. The fifty, you mean? (*She nods, he continues with gentle raillery*) Don't reckon I'd better, Emma. Start takin' oscar from wimmen and don't know where you'll end.

EMMA (*Shrewdly*).   You can't kid me. 'S not enough, is it?

ROO.   Well, it'd last a couple of weeks, I s'pose. Layin' off, you go through a lot.

EMMA.   Not a lot of mine, you don't. Fifty's as far as I'd trust you. And you're about the only bloke I'd trust with that much.

ROO (*Sincerely*).   I know. You're a real pal, Emma. But there's no reason why you should trust me any more than you would —Barney.

EMMA (*Bluntly*).   Don't be silly. I've trusted you with Olly all these years, haven't I?

ROO.   Have you?

EMMA.   Ever since she brought you in and introduced us standin' in that hall. You pushed back your hat and grinned at me. I summed you up right there and then—a packet of trouble, but he's honest—

ROO (*Wryly*).   Trouble, anyway.

EMMA.   It could have been worse. Seventeen years is seventeen years, even though they ain't nothin' but the lay-off season. But if you don't take the money, what'll you do?

ROO.   I can always get a job.

EMMA.   In the city?

ROO.   Would it surprise you? (*She nods emphatically*) Well, be prepared, 'coz that's what I'm goin' after.

EMMA (*Marveling*). Talk about throwin' bombshells! I can't wait for this. . . . (*She starts to exit, encountering* BARNEY *as he comes downstairs*) Here, you, if you want any breakfast, you'd better get a move on. . . .

BARNEY (*Pleasantly*). Ah, shut your face.

EMMA (*Exiting*). Righto. You can just go flamin' well without for that. See if you don't.
> (BARNEY *is wearing a shirt that he has obviously been to bed in, a baggy-kneed pair of pants sagging under his paunch, and a sloppy pair of slippers. He wanders down, bleary-eyed and yawning.*)

BARNEY. Sleepin' on that sofa's no joke. I'm gunna tell Olive.

ROO. She knows. You made enough fuss about it last night.

BARNEY (*Sitting*). Oh. Y'heard, did yer?

ROO. Couldn't help it. Lammin' away at that door.

BARNEY. What d'yer mean, lammin'? Just tapped light with me fingernails.

ROO. Well, whatever it was, she didn't like it.

BARNEY. Oh, I'm a wake up what's wrong with her. Did Olive tell you?

ROO. Yeh.

BARNEY. You know who she reminds me of? That little blond woman had a shop in Townsville. What was her name? Dowson—Dawson.

ROO. Donovan. Somehow I don't reckon you're gunna get around this one.

(ROO *throws envelope containing snapshots onto table.*)

BARNEY. Give us a go. I haven't had a talk to her yet. (*Sees envelope*) What's that?

ROO. Bubba brought them in for yer, some snaps of Nancy's weddin'. You're not to show Olive.

(BARNEY *opens envelope, takes out first photographs, looks at them for long moment, then speaks unemotionally.*)

BARNEY. She must have been ravin' mad. (*He shoves photos into pocket*) What's there in the paper?

ROO. Nothin' much. All down south.

BARNEY (*Leafing through*). It would be. How we goin' to fill in the day?

ROO. Well, I dunno about you, but I'm goin' lookin' for work. (BARNEY *is jolted into attention.*)

BARNEY (*Amazed*). But this is the lay-off. You can't go lookin' for work in the lay-off!

ROO. I told you on the plane when I got down here I'd get a job.

BARNEY. Yeh, I know, but I thought once you were here—and with Olly—

ROO. Leave Olive out of it.

47

BARNEY.   Well, me, then. I got money.

ROO.   I don't want your money, I can still earn my own. (*Bitingly*) Even if I have got a busted back.

BARNEY (*Stung*).   You pig-headed mug. What about all those times you've carried me—every year when I've run dry down here you've kicked me on . . .

ROO.   Yeh, well, this time you'd better hang on to what you've got for as long as you can. That won't be happenin'.

BARNEY.   It's all that lousy rotten pride of yours, ain't it? You're crook on me because I stayed up there with Dowdie and didn't walk out with you.

ROO.   I'm not crook on anythin'.

BARNEY.   Oh, yes, you are. You got a snout on that kid the first day you saw him workin'.

ROO (*Intensely*).   Cut it out . . .

BARNEY.   I watched yer! The morning after you turned poor old Tony Moreno off. . . .

ROO (*Furiously*).   Cut it out or I'll bash your face in!
(*There is a silence for a second or two, then* BARNEY *turns away and picks up paper, speaking in low, bitter resignation.*)

BARNEY.   Righto. You go and get yourself a job. See if I care. I'll find some way of amusin' meself.
(ROO *turns his back on him;* OLIVE *enters briskly.*)

OLIVE.   What's up with you two?

ROO (*Mumbling as he moves to arch*).   Ah—just arguin' the point.
> (*He exits upstairs.* OLIVE *glances after him a shade impatiently.*)

OLIVE.   Can't you ever give it a rest? (*She comes into room, speaking rapidly*) Barney, look, it's time me and Pearl left for the pub. She doesn't want to talk to you, but I've persuaded her into it. Now be careful what you say, 'coz she's just about ready to ring a taxi truck to pick up her things. Smooge round her a bit. . . .

BARNEY (*Sullenly*).   Ah, if she wants to go, let her go.

OLIVE.   Like hell we will. I've worked hard on this, explainin' things, gettin' her interested—what's wrong with you?

BARNEY.   Roo's goin' out to get himself a job.

OLIVE.   What?

BARNEY.   A job.

OLIVE (*Startled*).   When?

BARNEY.   Right now.

OLIVE (*Angrily*).   Oh, no. No, he mustn't . . . (*She hastens up the stairs, passing* PEARL *on the landing, calling*) Roo . . .
> (*After her exit* BARNEY *mooches over to French window, stands looking out.* PEARL, *a little bewildered, appears in archway. She hesitates, then speaks tentatively.*)

PEARL.   Barney . . .

BARNEY (*Turning*). Oh. G'day, Pearl. Come on in.

PEARL (*Nervously*). Shut the window, will you? I want to talk to you.

BARNEY. A bit shy, eh? (*He closes window*) Well, I can understand that.
> (*He smiles vaguely at her. It must be understood here* BARNEY's *instinct for wooing is mechanically reacting at the beginning of this scene, his mind is on other things. Later on, however, he becomes genuinely interested.*)

PEARL. Olive's asked me . . .

BARNEY (*Interposing*). Wait a minute, first I got to apologize to yer. Roo sez I kicked up a row outside your door last night.

PEARL. Don't you remember?

BARNEY. Well, this p'bably sounds like a bit of bull, but I don't. Most likely it was all that beer I put away, then it bein' my first night down here, and Nancy always havin' had that room other times . . .
> (*He allows a delicate pause.*)

PEARL. Yes-es. But it was my name you kept yellin' out.

BARNEY. Was it?

PEARL. Pearlie, you kept sayin', it's me, Pearl.

BARNEY. That's interestin'. Even when I didn't know what I was doin', I could still remember your name. Just shows you what an impression you must have made on me.

PEARL (*Still suspicious*).   Umm, I don't think you can judge by that. Anyway, it's not what I've come to see you about. Olive said I ought to . . .

BARNEY (*Quickly*).   Yeh, she told me, too—we're to have a quiet little chat. That the idea? Well, there's no reason why you should stand up for it, is there? Take the weight off your feet.
(*He places a chair for her. She hesitates for a moment, and then sits gingerly. He has robbed her of the advantage of a firm opening, and she now starts a little uncertainly.*)

PEARL.   It's no business of mine, you understand, and you might reckon I've got a bit of a cheek, but there's somethin' Olive didn't tell me when she first asked me if I'd like to be— (*Choosing the word carefully*) a friend of yours.

BARNEY.   Kept somethin' back, did she?

PEARL.   Yes. (*Girding herself*) Like I say, it's really no business of mine, but until last Saturday I didn't know you had any— de facto wives.

BARNEY.   But I haven't! Ooh, what you mean is my kids? (*She nods stiffly*) I tipped it'd be that. Yes, kids I got all right. In three states.

PEARL (*Swallowing hard*).   Well, that's it. I didn't want to have to talk to you about it, but Olive said I couldn't walk out without tellin' you, so . . .
(*She makes a move as if to rise; he checks her.*)

BARNEY. Hold on a bit . . . did she tell you the rest of it? That I paid maintenance on every one of them till they got old enough to work—that I'm still payin' for the youngest girl?

PEARL (*Bursting in*). Maintenance! Do you reckon that's the only claim they've got on you? Honest, when I think what their mothers must have gone through! I'm a mother myself, I can . . . (*Words fail her.*)

BARNEY. You're real mad at me, aren't yer?

PEARL. Yes, I am. There's no excuse for that sort of thing, you're just a no-hoper. You must be!

BARNEY (*Sincerely*). Maybe I am. But I can't help it. Honest. Ever since I was a kid, whenever I've met a good-lookin' woman, I've always felt like an excited eel in a fish basket.

PEARL. Don't make jokes about it.

BARNEY. I'm not. I know it's nothin' to be proud of—but I'm not gunna apologize for it, either.

PEARL (*Outraged*). And that's that! Just sayin' you're weak gives you the right to run around and have kids wherever you want to—

BARNEY. No, it doesn't. But the ordinary bloke's got a way out, he can get married. There's always been a sorta reason why I never could. . . .

PEARL (*Incredulously*). With children in three states? I'd like to hear of any reason that big!

BARNEY (*Bluntly*). Righto then—you listen. My eldest boys, the two of 'em, are both about the same age.

PEARL. Well?

BARNEY. Well, use your nut, don't you see what it means? Their mothers was in trouble at the same time. Oh, I'm to blame for that, and I'm not sayin' I ain't, but I was only a silly kid when it happened. Eighteen, I was.

PEARL. Old enough to face up to your responsibilities.

BARNEY. Maybe it is, but it's hardly old enough to face up to a big decision like—which of the two was I s'posed to marry? You just think of it—two good decent girls, and you can only make it right for one of them. I nearly went mad. Whichever one of them I married, I thought it'd be a rotten insult to the other. And it would have been. Both of them said so.

PEARL (*Dogged*). You could have done somethin'.

BARNEY. What? (*She is stumped for an answer*) Anyway, I didn't have time. My old man found out about it, and he kicked me out. Gave me a quid and a blanket, nearly twelve o'clock at night. Little place called Makarandi it was, up in New South. Well, that settled it. I knew I 'ad to make some big money fast, so I went where the big money was, then —off to Queensland.

PEARL. What you mean is, you run out on the girls!

BARNEY. I was doin' the best I could for everyone. I put me age up to twenty-one, and I worked like a Trojan. Paid all their bills right through, I did, everythin' for both of them. And after that I started payin' maintenance. But I left it up to them which one I was to marry. You decide, I said. (*With long-remembered relish*) Well—they're sittin' up there in that little one-horse town in New South Wales still arguin' about it! And I'm as far off marriage as ever I was—'coz if there's one thing I do believe in, it's first come, first served!

PEARL (*Confused*). That's all very well, but it doesn't excuse your—other mistakes. While you was waitin' you should have behaved yourself.

BARNEY. Pearl, those eldest boys of mine are old enough to vote now.

PEARL. Even so, I think it's criminal, real criminal. That's the only word for it.

BARNEY. Crim'nal, my eye. I've never had a complaint lodged against me in my life—official, that is. (*Amusedly—sitting*) You're talkin' as if I've got a string of ruined wimmen behind me. I haven't. One by one they've all settled down, pretty happy, too. Even that first pair up in Makarandi. I'll guarantee if I was to go back there now and try to break up their argument by marryin' one of them—they'd both join together and cut me throat. No, I tell yer, if there's anyone left out in the cold as the result of what I've done, it's no one but meself.

PEARL (*Sternly*). Nothin' more than what you deserve. Not that you have been much out in the cold, if what Olive tells me is true.

BARNEY. Olive! Aah, to listen to her you'd reckon I was the biggest Cassa in the North. It ain't as bad as that, you know.

(*Consideringly*) Still, most places I've gone, in between, I have been pretty lucky.

PEARL. That's what you call it, is it?

BARNEY. Lucky? Yeh. You know why? (*She shakes her head*) It takes a special sort of woman to understand a bloke like me. Most of them hear a thing or two and then get a set on yer, treat you as if you was poison.

PEARL. Can you blame them?

BARNEY. No, I don't. They dunno no better, see. But every now and then you meet a woman who does. She takes a tumble that a feller might have done a bit of chasin' around, not 'coz he was after all the lovin' he could get, but because he had a lot of lovin' that he could give. That's a hell of a difference most wimmen can never cotton on to.

PEARL (*Slowly*). No. I don't suppose they can.

BARNEY. That's why I say a man's lucky when he meets up with one of the other sort. . . .

PEARL (*Thoughtfully*). Chases round not because he's what?

BARNEY. After all the lovin' he can get . . .

PEARL. But because he's got a lot of lovin' he can give? That right?

BARNEY. Yeh. Sounds simple 'nuff, doesn't it. Yet you'd be surprised how few wimmen can cop on to it. Takes so many things, see. (*With fine concentration*) She's got to have experience, f'rinstance, so she can spot this kind of bloke from the mob. Then she's got to be able to take him for what he is, not try to tie him down . . . (OLIVE, *wearing hat and carrying bag, appears in archway*) And last of all, of course, she's got to have . . . (*He sees* OLIVE *and breaks off*) Well, never mind that now, here's Olive.

(*They look up at* OLIVE *as she stands, sulky dejection in every line of her figure.*)

OLIVE. You better get your things, Pearl. We're late.

PEARL (*Slowly—to* BARNEY, *after rising*). What's she got to have last of all?

BARNEY. Tell you some other time. You gotta hurry.
(*She gives him a look of curious disappointment and moves up to exit, speaking to* OLIVE *as she does so.*)

PEARL. Won't be a minute, luv.
(*She exits.*)

BARNEY (*Rising—anxiously to* OLIVE). Any luck with Roo?
(*She shakes her head*) He's really going out now to get himself a job?

OLIVE. Yes.
(*She moves moodily out to appear on front veranda, leaving door open behind her. In the room,* BARNEY *curses violently under his breath, flings himself into chair.* ROO *comes downstairs, dressed, but with no tie, and with his coat hanging over one shoulder.*)

ROO (*Calling toward veranda*). Olive?

OLIVE (*Looking back, disagreeably*). What?

ROO. I'll walk you and Pearl down to the tram. . . .

OLIVE. Well, I'm ready.

ROO (*Looking into room at* BARNEY). Hurroo. I might be back later and I might not.

(BARNEY *turns his back, offended.* ROO *moves out to join* OLIVE *on the veranda.* EMMA's *voice lets fly offstage.*)

EMMA (*Off*). Hey, you're not goin' out, are yer? What about your breakfast?

ROO (*Calling back*). I don't want any.

EMMA (*Appearing from kitchen*). After me slavin' me inside out cookin' it? Who else is gunna eat steak at this hour of the day?

ROO. Give it to Barney.

EMMA. Throw it over next door to the dog, that's what I ought to do. (*She looks into room at* BARNEY) And you, yer lazy sod, lollin' there. Git on out into the kitchen.

BARNEY (*Unmoving*). Don't you order me around.

EMMA. Order yer 'round? I'll chuck the teapot over yer in a minute. (*Vengefully, for both their benefits*) You just wait till tomorrow mornin', see how far you go then. There's gunna be a few changes made 'round here.

(*With a nod of dire warning, she exits again into kitchen.* OLIVE *moves to front door to yell.*)

OLIVE. Peeeaaarl.

PEARL (*Offstage*). I'm comin'. (*There is a slight pause, during which* OLIVE *shifts back to her place, then* PEARL, *a little breathless, wearing hat, carrying bag, and drawing on gloves, appears in archway. She smiles, hesitates, and speaks to* BARNEY *in what amounts to a girlish flutter*) Well, I'm off now.

BARNEY (*Looks at her and turns away*). Oh—ta ta.

PEARL. I was thinkin'—if you haven't much to do today—

BARNEY. Yeh?

PEARL. You might like to take my bags upstairs. (*He looks back with a broad grin, and she amends hastily—*) But don't jump to any conclusions, there's nothin' settled yet!

BARNEY (*Rising*). You little beaut! Listen . . .

PEARL (*Nervously escaping*). No, I'll—I'll see you tonight. 'Bye 'bye.

BARNEY. Pearl. . . .
(*But she has swooped out to* OLIVE *on the front veranda.* BARNEY *follows to door.*)

PEARL (*Breathlessly*). Well—are we all ready? Let's go then, eh? (*As they move off*) Lucky you're so close to the trams, Ol. . . .
(BARNEY *is standing looking after them and laughing as* ROO *moves out from the veranda shadows to follow. Their glances hold for a second, and the little man's laughter dies away as* ROO *steps down from the veranda and exits.* BARNEY *closes the front door abruptly, and leans with his back against it.*)

BARNEY (*Bitterly*).   Dirty lousy rotten pride.

   (PEARL'S *cases, standing prominently in the hall, catch his eye, and a weak grin slides across his face. Self-esteem returns, and with an overdone jaunty swagger he picks them up, squares his shoulders to the burden, and starts to run upstairs.*)

Curtain

ACT TWO

ACT TWO

Scene One

Time: New Year's Eve.

It is a warm summer night. The lighting on veranda and outside the house is a darkness of exhausted heat. Inside the room it is an electric, sweat-reflecting pink. The French windows and front door are open in the hope of catching any stray breeze that might spring up, but a general feeling of stillness prevails.

OLIVE *and* ROO *are playing cards. She is in an old dirndl and slippers, he in drab shirt and pants.* PEARL, *more formally dressed than* OLIVE, *is wearing a bright print with a dominant note of red—both of* PEARL's *outfits in Act Two reflect her fling at the gay life. She is sitting on the rocker, knitting.* BARNEY *is laboriously finishing off a letter. A contrast must be made between* ROO *and* BARNEY. ROO, *though dressed meanly, has the scrubbed look of a man who has showered well after a day's work. On the other hand,* BARNEY, *though seen in open-necked silk shirt and sports slacks, gives an impression of hot, gritty disagreeableness —the aftermath of a heavy day's drinking. He is not, however, by any means drunk. Throughout this scene, at appropriate moments, the distant and various sounds of New Year's revelry are faintly audible. At curtain rise this is most noticeable in the lost, drawn-out cries of children at some late street game. Hearing,* PEARL *looks toward the windows and smiles comfortably. It should be noted here that* PEARL *has blossomed; from the*

63

suspicious tentative approach she had in Act One, she has graduated to an assurance that is a little offensive in its complacency.

PEARL. Listen to the kids. (*There is no response, and she adds meaninglessly*) We used to play that—Charlie over the Water, it's called. (*A clock chimes the half-hour somewhere, and* BARNEY *and* OLIVE *exchange a look; then from her knitting* PEARL *looks across at* BARNEY) Have you put in what I said about havin' her trained for dressmakin'?

BARNEY. Ah, get off me back, will you. They'd reckon I was mad.

PEARL. 'Bout time you took some sort of interest. Dear May, here's the usual, hope you're both well— Hardly call that havin' a family.

BARNEY. Who said it was? I haven't got a family, what I got is kids. (*He slaps viciously at his arm*) Bloody mossies!

ROO. It's them ferns on the veranda. Full of 'em.

OLIVE. I call trumps.

BARNEY (*Irritably pleading*). Let's get away out of it, then, eh? Go down the beach or somewhere.

PEARL. Oh, it's too late now. Half-past eleven.

BARNEY. On New Year's Eve? How late's that? Even the nippers are still runnin' the streets.

OLIVE. It's all right for you, you haven't been workin' all day. Spades.

BARNEY.   Well, no one's gunna sleep anyway, a night like this. (*He licks and seals envelope with a thump*) We might as well be down there as stewin' here, gettin' eaten alive.

PEARL.   You're always wantin' to be goin' out somewhere.

BARNEY.   Not only me, what about Olly?

OLIVE (*Flatly*).   I'm playin' cards.

BARNEY.   Other times it used to be you draggin' us down to the beach on hot nights. (*Reminiscently*) 'Member when we hired the old bloke with the cab to take us down to Altona? We got home half-past seven in the morning. You didn't worry about workin' all day then.

PEARL.   Oh, shut up, Barney. Can't you see no one wants to go. Roo's tired.

ROO (*Jerking his head up*).   Who—me? I'm not tired. You don't have to stay home on my account. . . .

OLIVE.   'Course we don't. I just couldn't be bothered, that's all.

BARNEY.   Well, what are we gunna do, then?

PEARL.   I know. (BARNEY *looks up expectantly*) Come and let me try this sleeve on you.

BARNEY.   What the hell for? He's three inches taller 'n me, and bigger. . . .

PEARL.   Doesn't matter, it gives us some idea.

BARNEY (*Rising*). Oh, Gawd.
(*He slouches over to her, and she goes through the sleeve-measuring routine.*)

PEARL. Hold it there. (*He shifts it up to his shoulder*) No, there. (*Brings the bottom edge to his wrist*) Now bend your elbow—

OLIVE. Who's it for?

PEARL (*Maternally*). The eldest, Lennie.

BARNEY (*Correctingly*). One of the eldest. (*Looking down*) Not even long enough for me yet.

PEARL (*Turning back to piano to consult a pattern book, and stretching the knitting a little*). Well, at least I know.

BARNEY (*Putting letter and writing things on sideboard*). Kiddin' there's not goin' to be some ructions in Turrow once that turns up.

PEARL. Why should there be? Soon's I've finished this I'll start on one for Arthur.

BARNEY. Arthur—Chippa, they call him. (BUBBA, *wearing a simple white evening gown, appears to him on back veranda*) Well, here's somebody goin' out to celebrate, anyway.

BUBBA (*Questioningly*). Olive? I said I'd show Olive my dress.

OLIVE (*Calling from room*). Come on in, luv . . . (BUBBA *enters*) Well now, isn't that somethin'!

BARNEY (*Appreciatively*). Yeh. Row for the shore, boys.

BUBBA (*Pleasurably confused*).   That's enough, Barney. . . .

PEARL (*Undoing a skein of wool*).   Where are you goin', Bubba?

BUBBA.   One of those social-club dances. Some of the girls from work asked me.

ROO.   You've left it a bit late, haven't you?

BUBBA.   Oh, they're no fun till half-past eleven, I don't mind being late. (*Hesitatingly*) 'Fact, I'd just as soon not go at all. Dances on New Year's Eve get pretty silly, and when it's so hot like this . . . (*Her voice trails off, and then she makes a hopeful bid*) I wouldn't mind just stayin' home and playin' cards.

OLIVE.   In that dress? Don't be silly. 'Sides, what about those other girls, won't they be waitin' for you?

ROO.   You'll enjoy yourself once you get there.

BARNEY.   Yeh. And who knows—maybe tonight's the night! (*He makes a bawdy clicking sound with his tongue.*)

BUBBA (*Laughing despite herself*).   You fool, Barney. This place, it's just about the dullest you could find. (*After a pause, during which she looks them over uncertainly*) Aren't you goin' out anywhere at all?

BARNEY.   Naah. (*Looking over at* PEARL *untangling wool*) We're havin' one of them sensational at-home parties.

BUBBA (*Impulsively*).   You could've gone to the Morrises', y'know. I'll bet they wouldn't have minded a scrap. . . .

BARNEY (*Hopefully*). That's what I said.

BUBBA. Even now, if you hurried. . . .

OLIVE (*Finally*). Bubba, once and for all, we are not goin' to the Morrises'.

BUBBA. Oh.

PEARL (*After a short pause*). Who are the Morrises?

ROO (*Kindly, to* BUBBA). You'd better hop off, kid. You're late.

BUBBA. Yes. I s'pose I'd better wish you all Happy New Year now. (*She is answered with an overlapping confusion of greetings*) And I'll see you tomorrow.
(*She moves to the window.*)

BARNEY (*Kissing her and moving up with her*). Yeh, but you're not leavin' that dance till sunup, so don't you go comin' in here too early.

BUBBA (*Smiling*). All right, 'bye.

BARNEY. 'Bye 'bye, Bub.
(*She exits. There is a pause within room, then* PEARL *inquires, overcasually—*)

PEARL. Who did you say the Morrises were?

ROO (*Shuffling cards*). It's a place we used to go to for New Year parties.

PEARL (*Suspiciously*). Nobody's mentioned that one before. Why aren't you goin' this year?

OLIVE (*Exploding*). 'Cause the Morrises are cousins of Nancy's, that's why.

(*Conscious of having made a gaffe,* PEARL *shrugs and starts to wind the new skein into a ball.* BARNEY *eyes* OLIVE, *understanding her mood, and comes down quickly, definitely determined to change the subject.*)

BARNEY (*To* PEARL). Here, let me give you a hand with that wool. (*He sits, takes wool over his outstretched hands and holds it for* PEARL *to wind*) Y'know, it's a funny thing. All the wimmen I've ever knocked around with, there's never been one of them ever knitted anythin' for me. Now, why d'yer reckon that is?

OLIVE. They didn't have time, p'bably.

BARNEY. No, they didn't want to. I think it's a kinda compliment. Some fellers bring out the knittin' in wimmen, and some don't. I don't.

PEARL (*With a trace of malice*). Well, after all, who wants to knit a sweater for a bird of paradise.

BARNEY. A what?

PEARL. Oh, nothin'. It's just somethin' Olive said once.

BARNEY. What was it?

PEARL (*Coyly*). Can I tell 'em, Olive?

OLIVE. I don't remember callin' him no bird of paradise.

PEARL. You did. After that big fat bloke from the *Herald* had been tellin' us about them birds that fly from place to place. . . .

OLIVE (*Embarrassed*). Oh, that! You don't have to drag that up.

BARNEY (*Out for fun*). Yes, she does. Go on, Pearl. What'd she say?

PEARL (*Winding wool, unaware of the havoc she is to create*). Well, it was in the early part, when she first started to tell me about you two. We'd been talkin' one morning, she was tryin' to describe how she felt about youse comin' down every year, when in walks this fat feller. Real ear-basher he is, always on for a yap. This particular time he gets gassin' about birds, sayin' how some of them fly all over the place, spend a season here and a season there, sort of thing. Well, me, I couldn't have cared less what they did, but Olly got real wrapped up in it. After a while she turned to me and said . . .

OLIVE (*Interrupting*). It was when he'd gone, I didn't say it in front of him.

PEARL. When he'd gone, then, she turned to me and said— (*Pauses enjoyably*) What was it? Oh yes—that's what they remind me of, she sez, two birds of paradise flyin' down out of the sun and comin' south every year for the matin' season. (*She goes off into a smother of mirth and resumes winding wool. The other three are not amused.*)

OLIVE (*Sharply*). It might sound silly when you put it like that, but it fitted in with what he'd been sayin'!

PEARL (*Gurgling*). Yes—but birds of paradise! (*To the men*) Honest, she boosted you two up so much before you came, I didn't know what to expect—

OLIVE. It wasn't as bad as that.

PEARL (*In superior smugness*). Oh, yes, it was, Olly; I don't think you realized. The way you went on about everythin'—sounded just as if when they arrived the whole town was gunna go up like a balloon.

OLIVE. When did I say that?

PEARL. It was how you talked all the time. Look what you said about them Sunday-night boat trips up the river. Beautiful, you said.

OLIVE. Well, was it my fault it rained?

PEARL. No, but even if it hadn't—that terrible old boat—

OLIVE. You didn't give it a fair go.

PEARL (*On her mettle*). All right then, what about Christmas at that week-end place in Selby? You can't say I didn't give that a fair go.

BARNEY (*Staring*). And what was wrong with Selby?

PEARL (*Largely*). Oh, it wasn't bad, but the way she cracked it up, I expected a palace. . . .

ROO (*Truculently*). You wouldn't find a better little place than that this side of Sydney.

PEARL. Oh, get away with you. It hasn't even got electricity.

OLIVE (*Slapping her cards down and rising angrily*). Look, what are you tryin to do? Make out I'm a liar or somethin'?
(PEARL *ceases to wind, surprised*.)

PEARL. I didn't say a liar. . . .

71

OLIVE. Then don't say anythin', 'coz that's what it sounds like.

PEARL (*Disdainfully*). I was only tellin' you how the whole thing looked to me. If a person can't pass an opinion . . .

OLIVE. You pass too many damned opinions, that's your trouble.

ROO (*Soothingly*). Come on, Ol, finish your hand.

OLIVE (*Moving away abruptly*). Oh, I'm sick of cards. This waitin' up for twelve o'clock is just plain silly, I think I'll go to bed.
(*She starts toward stairs.*)

BARNEY (*Galvanizing into action and heading her off*). No, you can't. Look, I'll tell you what: we'll make it a party, get Emma in and have a sing-song—

ROO. She wouldn't play. You know what she said last time . . .

BARNEY (*Moving out onto front veranda*). She'll play. (*Calling*) Emma, what're you doin' out there?

EMMA (*A voice from the darkness*). Gettin' a sea breeze off the gutter. What d'yer think?

BARNEY. Want to earn ten bob?

EMMA. How?

BARNEY. Playin' the piano while we have a sing-song.

EMMA. No.

BARNEY (*Determinedly, after a glance back through the window into the room*). I'll make it a quid.

EMMA (*Suspiciously*). Who picks the chunes?

BARNEY. You can. Anythin' you want to.

OLIVE (*Calling sharply*). Don't tell her that—

BARNEY. Ssshh.

EMMA (*Reluctantly*). Righto. Get yourselves organized, and no muckin' about.

BARNEY (*Returning to room, happily*). C'mon—girlies on the sofa. Roo, get your chair—
(*During the next few lines* EMMA *makes her way across the veranda and into the house.*)

OLIVE (*As they arrange themselves*). You know what we're in for, don't you? She'll start off with "Goldmine in the Sky," and finish up with "Old Black Joe."

BARNEY. Doesn't matter. If it gets too slow we can always pep it up a bit—

ROO. With Emma? I'll bet you don't.

OLIVE. I'll bet you don't either.
(EMMA *enters from hallway, stands frowning in the light.*)

EMMA. Who's gunna pay the quid?

BARNEY. I am. But you've gotta do the job first. No walkin' out in the middle of it.

EMMA (*Walking to piano*). The only time I walk out on singin' is when there's muckin' about and youse don't take it serious. . . .

73

(*She removes a ring and places it ostentatiously on top of the piano.*)

BARNEY.   We're gunna take it serious this time.

EMMA.   You'd better. (*She seats herself at the piano, raises flap, massages her fingers*) Righto, on your feet, the lot of yer. (*All rise but* PEARL.)

PEARL (*A mite sulkily*).   Do I have to join in?

EMMA.   Well, it's community singin', ain't it? (PEARL *rises with a martyred air*) We'll start off with "Goldmine in the Sky."

OLIVE (*To* BARNEY).   There y'are, what did I tell you?

EMMA.   What d'yer mean, what did you tell him?

OLIVE.   Nothin'. I just said you'd start off with "Goldmine in the Sky," that's all.

EMMA.   I always start off with "Goldmine."

OLIVE (*Crossly*).   Nobody's kickin' about it, I just said you would.

EMMA.   It's me favorite.

OLIVE.   All right then, play the bloody thing!
(EMMA *gives her a wrathful look, and mutters something under her breath as she plays a short introduction. When this is over, she launches into song with a cracked, untrained, but surprisingly true voice. The others make a very ragged beginning, and she breaks off sharply*)

EMMA.   Righto, righto, that's the note to come in. (*She hits it a few times emphatically*) Try it again.

(OLIVE *sits on sofa despondently,* BARNEY *kneels behind her and pats her shoulder.* EMMA *leads them into song again, and this time the results are happier. They all sing except* PEARL, *who looks them over with a curled lip.*)

ALL. *There's a goldmine in the sky,*
Far away;
We will find it, you and I,
Some sweet day. . . .
(*But* EMMA *has broken off and is voicing fierce objections.*)

EMMA. Wait a minute, someone's singin' a bit flat. Listen— (*Singing*) ". . . We will find it . . ." (*Breaks off*) See? Try it again.
(*They do as requested.*)

ALL. . . . We will find it, you and I . . .

EMMA (*Interrupting*). No, no, no, it's still wrong. Sounds like a woman's voice . . .
(*She glares at* PEARL, *who turns away, livid with irritation.*)

OLIVE (*Impatiently*). Well, what's it matter? Get on with it.

EMMA. Flat?

BARNEY (*Forcefully*). Look, we're not after a singin' lesson, Emma; all we want's a bit of fun. . . .

EMMA. That's what I say—muckin' about, and you don't care whether you get it right or not.

75

OLIVE. How d'yer know it's not you that's wrong?

EMMA (*Rising, awfully*). I never sung a wrong note in me life. . . .

OLIVE. Who sez?

EMMA. Ask anybody at the community—ask Mr. Munro—

BARNEY. And what would he know about it?

EMMA. He's the conductor, ain't he? D'yer reckon he'd get me to sing a solo every year for me birthday if I sung it flat?

OLIVE. Does it for a laugh, p'bably.

EMMA. That's a flamin' lie and you know it. I'll bring him 'round here. . . .

ROO. You silly old rabbit, they're only pullin' your leg.

EMMA. Oh, so that's what you got me in for, is it—to poke mullock?

BARNEY (*Hitting a note*). You was asked in to play the pianner—

EMMA (*Crowing vehemently*). Yeh—for a single fiddlie! (*She bangs the flap down, replacing ring, and charges out angrily, throwing over her shoulder*) Well, I wouldn't listen to what youse call singin' for all the tea in China! Bunch of croakin' amachers!

(*The others are silent as she stumps across veranda, and then* PEARL *speaks, a touch satirically.*)

PEARL. Well, I suppose you could say that's one of the shortest community-singin' sessions on record.

OLIVE (*Disgustedly*). Aah, she gets worse all the time.

ROO (*Reprovingly*). You shouldn't have said that, 'bout them only gettin' her to sing for a joke.

OLIVE. Well, who does she think she is—Nellie Melba?

ROO. No, but her singin', that's one thing she's proud of.

OLIVE (*Firing up*). Look, she treads on my corns and she doesn't say she's sorry. Emma's got to learn to knuckle down a bit.

ROO (*Angrily*). Righto. Forget it!
(*He lies on the sofa.*)

BARNEY (*Another desperate attempt to save the situation*). Well, one thing anyway, it's—it's livened us all up. (*He throws a despairing glance at their unmoving figures, and appeals to* OLIVE) Look, before Pearlie gets back to her knittin', how about openin' up a few bottles, eh?

OLIVE (*Recklessly, rising*). Yes, what the hell, why not? It's New Year's Eve, ain't it? Come on, Pearl, we'll make some savories . . .
(*She crosses to hall.*)

PEARL (*Following her out to the kitchen*). I don't mind, anythin'—so long as we don't go down to the beach!
(*They have exited.* ROO *starts to roll a cigarette. The atmosphere between the men is that of a guarded truce, with* BARNEY *making a valiant pretense that no such bar exits.*)

BARNEY. That Emma, never thought I'd ever see the day she'd turn down a quid for anythin'.

ROO. She's always been fussy about singin'.

BARNEY (*Picking up letter from sideboard and crossing to mantelpiece, looking in vases*). Yeh, but why get so het up about it? She knows we was only on for a bit of fun. Wonder if Olive's got a stamp?

ROO. Better ask her.

BARNEY (*Putting letter in pocket*). Nah, it can wait. I oughta register it, anyway. (*Leading up to a tricky point*) How's the paint business?

ROO (*Indifferently*). Okay.

BARNEY (*Laughing a little forcedly*). I was thinkin' today, it won't be long before I'm down there with you, the way the money's runnin' out. . . .

ROO. Already?

BARNEY. You know me. If there's no one round to keep a check, I just throw it about.

ROO. Well, I warned yer, didn't I? You'd better not bank on gettin' in at Lyman's, it's a pretty small place.

BARNEY (*Hedging*). Oh, I can still hang on for a few weeks yet. Besides, that sort of joint, I'm not sure I'd be interested— (*With great animation, as if in sudden remembrance*) Oh, yeh, I didn't tell you, did I? Meant to when I got in. Some of the boys are down.

ROO (*Stiffening*). What boys?

BARNEY. The gang: Bluey, Freddie Waye—that lot. Got the shock of me life, walked into Young and Jackson's this mornin', and there they were, cocked up in the bar. Didn't know a word about it. They've come south for the fruit pickin', a course, and Bluey got 'em to take a coupla weeks off for a booze-up in town. . . .

ROO. And just by accident you bump into them at Young and Jackson's?

BARNEY (*Protestingly*). I been drinking there a lot lately, with you not around. What's the matter, d'you reckon I met 'em by 'pointment or somethin'?

ROO. I wouldn't be surprised.

BARNEY. Gawd, what a low suspicious sort of coot you are. Just by chance . . .

ROO. All right, no need to harp on it. What did they have to say?

BARNEY. Well, they wanted to know where you was, a course. I said you was workin', but I didn't tell 'em where.

ROO. I'll bet you didn't.

BARNEY. I didn't—I didn't think you'd want me to! 'Struth, don't you believe anythin' I tell you?

ROO. Not much. I been listenin' to you shovelin' it out for a long time, don't forget. What else did they say?

BARNEY (*Hurt*). Aahh—don't feel like tellin' you now. Just bits of stuff from up north. Oh—and they wanted to know if we'd go out with 'em on the tear sometime.

ROO. How about young Dowd?

BARNEY (*Cautiously*). Well, yes, he's with 'em, but there's a lot of . . .

ROO. There ain't no buts to it!

BARNEY (*Losing his temper*). S'help me, how long you gunna keep this up? He don't hold no grudges, he'd like to see you, he told me so. . . .

ROO. I don't want to see him.

BARNEY. Well, that puts me in a fine spot, doesn't it!

ROO. How the hell does it affect you? You wanta go, you go.

BARNEY (*Fiercely*). You know I wouldn't without you— (ROO *turns his head to look at* BARNEY *directly, and the little man wilts, then speaks quietly and honestly*) Righto—so I didn't walk out with you up north. But that was the only time I ever slipped. I've stood by you other times, haven't I?

ROO (*Away from him*). I didn't need you other times. That was once I did.

BARNEY. All right, I was in the wrong. But give me a chance to make it up, won't yer? Twenty years of knockin' around together, I oughta deserve that much.

ROO (*After a pause, softening*). What is it you want to do?

BARNEY (*Eagerly*). Help you to get back on top with the boys.

ROO. How?

BARNEY (*Joining him on sofa, the enthusiastic planner*). Well, you workin' in that paint dump and me with me money runnin' out, first of all I thought we might go up to the Murray with 'em for the grapes.

ROO (*Catching on to what* BARNEY *is scheming. In a stillness*). Walk out on Olive and Pearl? Is that what you want?

BARNEY. We could explain it to them. Gee, you can't say there's been much fun in it this time, you workin' and Nancy gone. . . .

ROO (*Rising, grimly*). I forgot. That's your rotten form, ain't it? Once the fun goes . . .

BARNEY (*Angrily*). Don't start on that, it's not like that at all. They're not enjoyin' it any more than we are.

ROO. Who sez they're not?

BARNEY. Oh, maybe Pearl thinks it's all right, but then she doesn't know what it used to be like before. . . .

ROO. And Olive?

BARNEY. Well, you could put it up to her, couldn't you? At least ask her!

ROO. You selfish little bastard! You listen to me—we come down here for the lay-off, five months of the year, December to April. That leaves another seven months still hangin'— what d'yer reckon Olive does in that time? Knocks around with other blokes, goes out on the loose every week? No, she doesn't, she just waits for us to come back again—'coz she thinks our five months is worth all the rest of the year put together! It's knowin' that that brought me down this time, broke and—and when I would have given anythin' to have stopped up there. But I couldn't let her down—and if I hear you mention either grapes or the Murray to her now, I'll kick you so far they'll have to feed you with a shanghai.

(BARNEY *shifts away, fights for composure, and then asks sorely—*)

BARNEY. What happens when me money runs out, then?

ROO. Get yourself a job somewhere.

BARNEY (*The final insult*). Like in a paint factory? Pigs I will!

ROO. Well, that's up to you—(*There is a rattle of trays offstage, and* PEARL *says "Oops, nearly lost the lot."* ROO *finishes quickly*) Now remember what I said.

(OLIVE *enters bearing tray with bottles of beer and glasses, followed by* PEARL, *carrying plates of sandwiches and savories*).

OLIVE (*Cheerfully*). We've just got time to pour 'em out before they start the sirens. (*Putting down the tray*). Come on, Barney, for once you can handle this lot. . . .

(*He moves, still disgruntled, to open bottles and pour glasses.* PEARL *places food on table.*)

PEARL. Hope yez all like mustard, I've laid it on. . . .

ROO. What about callin' Emma?

OLIVE. Oh, don't worry, she'll be in if she wants any. (*She comes to* ROO *and sits beside him*) I'm sorry, luv.

ROO. What for?

OLIVE. You know—all that moanin'.

PEARL (*Turning over savories*). Liverwurst, sardines, and cheese and gherkin—no one can say they haven't got a pick.

OLIVE (*Intimately, to* ROO). Can't think what got into me.

ROO. Who's worryin'?

BARNEY (*Gruffly, carrying glasses to them*). Here, wrap your fingers 'round these 'fore you start smoogin'.

PEARL (*Giggling as she fills glass for herself*). And this is the very last beer I pour this year.

OLIVE. We shoulda got a bottle of champagne or somethin'.

BARNEY (*Taking bottle from* PEARL). This is good enough for me.
  (*As he pours himself a glass there is a flash and whoosh from offstage.*)

ROO (*Crossing to window, pointing into night*). Hey, someone's lettin' off crackers—there's a rocket—put the lights off.
  (*This is done, and they are now lit by the fitful firework explosions offstage.*)

OLIVE. Gee, look at 'em! (*With spontaneous decision, turning back to* ROO) Y'know, I'm glad we didn't go out now—let the Morrises look after themselves, we're much better off on our own. Just the four of us here, and a few drinks to happy days.

BARNEY (*Half gay, half defiant*). That's it. Happy days 'n' (*Lifting glass to window*) glamorous nights!
  (PEARL, *who has been sneaking a sip of her beer, gives a whoop of mirth, choking herself on the swallow.*)

PEARL (*Gasping*). Ooh—oh, you fool, Barney, don't say things like that—

OLIVE. What?

PEARL. D-didn't you hear him?

BARNEY. All I said was . . .

PEARL (*Topping him*). Glamorous nights! I mean—look at us. (*She tries to catch her breath with another drink of beer, oblivious to the effect her words have had on the other three.* BARNEY *turns slowly to look at* ROO *and* OLIVE *in puzzled bewilderment, then* OLIVE'S *resolve breaks and she crumples down onto piano stool,* ROO *crouching beside her, trying wordlessly to comfort her.* BARNEY *turns his gaze from their naked misery and stares shamefacedly into his beer. Offstage, and far off, twelve great strokes announcing the New Year can be heard through the other celebration noises, which include a nearby house party singing "Auld Lang Syne," and distant cheering.*)

Curtain

SCENE TWO

Time: The following Friday evening.

It is about six-thirty, and the veranda is flooded with a fading sunlight that slowly, through this scene, takes on a deep blood tinge—a Russell Drysdale red—as the sun gradually sets. The French windows are closed, and the light is still strong enough to strike into the room.

At curtain rise, ROO, *dressed in paint-bespattered shirt and pants, is lying sprawled on the sofa, asleep. An evening paper lies beside him on the floor. The effect to be aimed at is that of a man caught up by tiredness after a heavy day's work. A taxi is heard driving up outside the house, and there follows a confused argument of drunken voices.*

BARNEY. Now, if we don't git our bowels in a knot, I'll have the whole thing settled in about two minutes flat—

DOWD (*Overlapping*). Nobody's got to worry about payin' this cab but me. 'Ere, mate, here's a quid—

BARNEY. Give 'im back his quid, or I'm gunna be real mad, I'm tellin' yer.
(OLIVE *mounts quickly up onto veranda, and pauses to call back.*)

OLIVE. Oh, stop your arguin'. It doesn't matter who pays him, just pay!
(*She opens front door, and* EMMA *hurries into view in hallway.*)

EMMA (*Hissing at* OLIVE). D'yer have to kick up all that row? Tell 'em to be quiet. Roo's asleep.

OLIVE. Asleep? (*Looking into room at* ROO.) Hasn't he even had a shower or anythin'?

EMMA. No. Just sat down to read the paper for a minute, 'n' he dozed off.

OLIVE (*Vexed*). You shouldna let him. (*She comes into room, calling*) Roo . . .

EMMA. Aah, leave him alone—(*But* OLIVE *is already shaking him awake. A fresh outburst of arguing from offstage takes* EMMA *out to investigate. As she exits*) Cut it out, can't yer? Roo's asleep.

BARNEY (*Off*). Emma—you come and settle this.

EMMA. Quiet!
    (*The noise outside ceases. Meanwhile, inside room—*)

OLIVE. Roo—wake up. (*He jerks into consciousness with a start*) C'mon, snap out of it.

ROO (*Sitting up, blinking*). What's the matter?

OLIVE. We're all home. You've been asleep.

ROO. Oh. (*Yawning*) Musta dozed off.

OLIVE. Yeh. Look, Barney's full and he's brought someone here to see yer, says he's a friend of yours—

ROO. Who?

OLIVE. I dunno. They was waitin' for us outside the pub with a taxi. Couldn't get much sense out of either of 'em, but I think he's from up north—

ROO (*Becoming alert*). What's he like?

OLIVE. Big bloke, dark. Have a look, they're arguin' in front over who's gunna pay the driver.
(ROO *crosses quickly to window and peers out. Turns back in slowly mounting fury.*)

ROO. I'll break his bloody neck for him—

OLIVE (*Tightly*). Who—who is it?

ROO. Young Dowd.
(*There is a short burst of male laughter offstage, and* BARNEY *crows, "Trust you to find a way out!"*)

OLIVE. I had a feelin'. (*Quickly*) Now listen, you don't have to see him, I'll stop him comin' in—

ROO. No, you can't do that—it's too late.

OLIVE. Why is it? We'll stop the taxi—

ROO. D'yer want him to think I'm scared? (*Taxi drives away offstage, cheered by* BARNEY) S'pose I'd have to meet him sometime, anyway.

OLIVE (*Anxiously*). Promise you won't start any blues, then?

ROO. That depends on him. (*A babble of voices starts to approach from the street*) Look at me.

OLIVE. Well, you haven't got time to change.

(EMMA *appears on front veranda, trying to drag away from* BARNEY, *who has hold of her apron. The strap at the back has been undone, and it is only held by the bib attachment at the nape of her neck.* DOWD *and* PEARL *have a grip on* BARNEY *and are trying to control him.*)

EMMA. You drunken sot! Why don't yer come home early for once?

BARNEY (*Whooping*). C'mon, Emma, you know you don't mean that. Give us a kiss.

EMMA. I'll do nothin' of the sort.

(BARNEY *makes a lunge at her.* PEARL *squeals "Barney," and* EMMA *retreats into the house.*)

DOWD (*Laughingly hanging on to* BARNEY). Let 'er go, Barney, she's too young, you'll get had up for carnival knowledge . . .

EMMA (*Firing back from stairs*). I don't know you. You keep a civil tongue in your head. . . .

BARNEY. C'mere, Emma, I'm not gunna hurt yer. . . .

OLIVE (*Trying to rivet their attention with a sharp command*). Barney, cut it out.

PEARL (*In relieved indignation, seizing his arm in fresh grip*). He's awful, you can't do a thing with him . . .

BARNEY. Lemme go!

(*He rips his arm brutally from her grasp, and his swing around with the action brings* DOWD *and him into the archway, facing* ROO *inside the room. They freeze, and*

88

there is a pause of complete waiting as they stare down at ROO, *who returns their gaze expressionlessly. Then* DOWD, *a big, boyish, friendly-looking fellow of twenty-five, obviously riding the crests of such waves as pride of body and unbroken spirit, speaks quietly.*)

DOWD. 'Lo, Roo.

ROO. 'Lo.

DOWD. Y'look like you been paintin' the town.

ROO. Yeh.

BARNEY (*Starting forward*). Roo, one thing you gotta . . .
(*But* DOWD *has reached a casual arm across and pushed him back beside* PEARL. *He now moves deliberately into the room to within four or five paces of* ROO *and holds out his hand.*)

DOWD. I wanna shake hands with you. (*Waiting*) Will you shake hands, Roo?
(ROO *pauses, then moves slowly in, looking directly into his face. His intention could just as easily be to kill as to comply with the request. When they are face to face,* ROO's *glance drops to the outstretched hand. Reluctantly, and clearly against his grain,* ROO *extends his own hand, and they shake.*)

BARNEY (*Elated, to* DOWD). Y'see, I told yer, that was all it needed—
(*He turns back to kiss* PEARL *sloppily, and she runs upstairs, disgusted.* BARNEY *staggers into the room, and* EMMA *takes the opportunity to escape into the kitchen.*)

DOWD (*Good-humoredly*). You shut up for a minute.

BARNEY. Just get youse face to face. . . .

DOWD (*Roughly*). Shut up! (BARNEY *lapses into hurt silence.* DOWD *turns to* ROO) Coupla things I got to tell you. First, I'm sorry I laughed that day—

ROO (*Mumbling*). Forget it.

DOWD. No, we won't, I shouldna done it. It was just that you looked pretty funny, down on your knees like that—

ROO (*Stupidly*). I slipped.

DOWD. Yeh. Well, I shouldna laughed. (*There is a faint, uneasy halt, then he continues jerkily*) That's one thing. The other's a sort of message from the boys—they want to see you. What about it? Tonight we're all goin' to the Stadium and we've got a coupla extra seats—

BARNEY (*Coming close to* DOWD). Ringside!
(ROO *moves his head helplessly, as though trying to evade a tightening trap.*)

ROO. I dunno about that—

DOWD. Why not?

OLIVE (*Cutting in swiftly and moving to* ROO). 'Coz he's made other arrangements, a course. What d'yer think?

BARNEY. Since when?

OLIVE. Never you mind.

DOWD (*Peaceably, after a shrewd glance at* OLIVE). Righto, then, how 'bout tomorrow afternoon? We'll take yer to the races—

ROO. Well—

BARNEY (*Encouragingly*). C'mon, you know you like the races.

DOWD. A day out with the boys, do you the world of good. . . .

OLIVE. I think I oughta have somethin'—

ROO (*Interrupting*). No, Olive! (*She falls silent, and he nods finally*) Okay. The races tomorrow afternoon.

DOWD (*Enthusiastically*). Fine! Now, where'll we meet? We'll hit the grog first, eh—

ROO. Whatever you like. You fix it up with Barney, I—I got to get out of these (*Indicating his clothes*) 'n' have a shower.

DOWD. Sure. (*As* ROO *goes toward stairs*) Looks like we caught you right home from work.

ROO (*Pausing stiffly, speaking out of a deep hurt*). Yeh.
(*He exits.* OLIVE *picks up gloves and bag, then inquires coldly—*)

OLIVE. Are you gunna eat with us, Mr. . . . ?

DOWD. Dowd, Johnnie Dowd's the name. (*Jerking his thumb at* BARNEY) I told this drunk he didn't introduce us. No, I gotta meet the boys at the London.

OLIVE. Just as well. Otherwise the drunk would 'ave to go out for more fish and chips.
(*She moves to exit upstairs, and* BARNEY *claps his hands above his head in a boxer's gesture of triumph.*)

BARNEY (*Delightedly*). Y'see. Easy as winkin'. I said it would work.

DOWD. Only just.

BARNEY. He shook hands, didn't he?

DOWD. Yeh. Like I was prickly pear.

BARNEY. Doesn't matter, he did it. I know Roo; once he's shook hands he'll start actin' right.

DOWD (*With a hint of a scowl*). He'd better. I don't mind sayin' I'm sorry to him, but that's all the crawlin' he's gunna get.

BARNEY. I'll bet tomorrow he'll be right as rain.

DOWD (*Unconvinced*). Yeh. (*He gives a short laugh and sits*) Maybe if we got really full together it'd patch things up.

BARNEY. That's what it needs, somethin' like that, gettin' full together.

DOWD. I'd like to make it right again. Pig-headed 'n' all as he is, I'm real fond of old Roo.

BARNEY. 'Course you are—after all, he turned off Tony Moreno to bring you in with us, didn't he? That's a big favor. And you know somethin' else—you and Roo have got a lot in common underneath, I been noticin' it more and more every day. (*An apparently sudden thought*) Hey, listen, I got an idea! All them fellers there tomorrer, you and Roo are hardly gunna have a word to say to one another. How 'bout, instead of a mob, we make it just the three of us—you, him, and me. Whaddya say?

DOWD (*Shaking his head*). No, he'd shut up like a clam on the both of us.

BARNEY (*Excitedly*). The sheilas then, Pearl 'n' Olive, we'll take them, too. That'll break the ice.

DOWD. And where do I come in?

BARNEY. Oh, that's all right, we'll fix you up with one as well.

DOWD. Not anythin' as old as them, you won't. I still got me own teeth, remember.

BARNEY (*Snapping his fingers*). I know what's for you—(*He lurches up to stairs and yells*) Pearlie—Pearl—
(DOWD *rises and crosses to fireplace, looking at room.*)

PEARL (*Offstage*). What d'yer want?

BARNEY. Come down here, wanna ask you somethin'. (*Re-entering room*) Just cracked on to the very thing. Piece about eighteen. That young enough for yer?

DOWD. What's she like?

BARNEY. Only seen her photo, but she looks terrific.

DOWD. You reckon she'd come?

BARNEY. Why shouldn't she?

DOWD. I dunno. (*A little awkwardly*) These young sheilas down south, a bit on the la-de-da side, ain't they?

BARNEY. All in the way you treat 'em. (PEARL *appears in arch-way*) Hullo, Pearl. C'mere, wanna talk to you. This young feller here, his name's Johnnie Dowd, he's a mate of ours from up north—

PEARL (*She walks past him and sits*). I know, Olive's been tellin' me.

93

BARNEY. Oh. Well, did she tell you the rest of it? That Roo and me are goin' to the races tomorrow with the boys?

PEARL. Yes.

BARNEY. Well, now Johnnie's come up with a better idea. (JOHNNIE *protests*) 'Stead of goin' out with all them blokes and gettin' full, he thinks it'd be nicer if the three of us took you and Olive.

PEARL (*Surprised*).   But me and Olive work Sat'day afternoons.

BARNEY. We can fix that, Olive'll ring 'em in the mornin', she's done it plenty of times before. But how'd you like it?

PEARL (*Uncertainly*).   'S long since I been. I always used to like the races. . . .

BARNEY (*Definitely*).   That's settled then, you're goin' tomorrer. You 'n' me, Roo 'n' Olive, and (*Turning significantly*) Johnnie.

PEARL. On his own?

BARNEY (*Smilingly seizing his opportunity*).   That's just what I wanted to talk to you about! Now, maybe I shouldn't say this in front of 'im, but for a young bloke this one here's pretty fussy where his wimmen are concerned. A bit on the shy side, see. . . .

DOWD. Hey, break it down. . . .

BARNEY. You keep out of it. (*He returns his attention to* PEARL, *coaxing her confidently*) So we just can't land him with anythin', 'n' I was thinkin'—how'd you like to bring that girlie of yours along—what's her name?

PEARL (*Alarmed*). Vera? To the races?

BARNEY. Yeh. Give her a day out.

PEARL. Oh, I couldn't, she's only eighteen.

BARNEY. Didn't you ever go to the races when you were eighteen?

PEARL. That's different. I didn't have a chance, from the beginnin'. I'm lookin' after Vera—she's not bein' brought up the way I was.

BARNEY. She's livin', ain't she? Walkin' round and breathin'?

PEARL (*Stiffly*). I won't have her goin' any place she's likely to get into bad company.

BARNEY (*To* DOWD, *marveling*). Will yer listen to that? Bad company! (*To* PEARL) I'm askin' her to go out with you (*He jabs her with his forefinger*)—her own mother!

PEARL. Not only me, there's others goin' too.

BARNEY. But you'll be there all the time. What's the matter, don't yer trust yourself to look after her?

DOWD (*Moving toward him—uneasily*). Barney, maybe it'd be better if we left it the way it was, just the blokes. . . .

BARNEY (*To* PEARL). There—did you hear that? The first time we really get a chance to make a splash, and you're gunna mess it up!

PEARL (*Near to tears*). Why should I let Vera go out with him? I dunno who he is. . . .

BARNEY. I told yer, he's a mate of mine. And she's not goin' out with him, she's goin' out with all of us. . . .

DOWD (*Worried, coming closer*). Barney, we'll make it just the blokes. . . .

BARNEY. No, we won't. By crikey, we won't. (*His face lights up*) Hey, hang on a bit, I know who to get. (*Diving for French windows*) You wait here. . . .
    (*He opens windows, passes out onto back veranda.*)

DOWD (*Following to window, a little amazed*). Barney . . . (*Realizing the hopelessness of trying to stop him, he turns to* PEARL) Where's he off to now?

PEARL (*Making toward arch*). How should I know? He can go to hell for all I care. . . .

DOWD (*With rough kindness*). Look, missus, if you don't want your daughter to go out with me, that's all right, I'm no baby snatcher. . . .

PEARL (*Working her way up to a crying jag*). Who does he think he is, tryin' on a trick like that?

DOWD. All he did was ask. . . .

PEARL. I know what he did, don't you tell me! Propositionin', that's what he was.

DOWD. I didn't hear nothin' about no propositions. . . .

PEARL. That's what you say. (*Making her way upstairs*) Tarred with the same brush, the lot of yer.
    (*She exits.* JOHNNIE *gives an exclamation of impatience, crosses to windows and calls urgently.*)

DOWD. Barney . . .

(*Immediately, but not in answer to* JOHNNIE'S *call,* BAR-
NEY *comes into view, talking to* BUBBA *as he pulls her
down the veranda.*)

BARNEY. . . . Drunk my eye, I gotta little surprise for yer.
Come on—

DOWD. Hey, that woman you left here, that Pearl, she's gone
all snaky. . . .

BARNEY. Ah, forget 'bout her. (*Drawing* BUBBA *into room*)
Here's the one I want you to meet. Bubba Ryan.

DOWD. How are yer?

BARNEY (*Standing behind her*). Oh, she's fine . . . aren't yer,
kid? You see this feller? Know where he comes from? (*She
shakes her head*) Way up north where the sugar grows. And
you want to know somethin' else? He's one of the best cutters
and . . .

(BUBBA'S *face lights with interest.*)

DOWD. All right, Barney, don't lay it on. (*Holding out his
hand*) Dowd's the name, miss—Johnnie Dowd.

BARNEY. See—he says it just as if it meant nothin' at all.

BUBBA (*Shaking hands shyly*). How d'you do?

BARNEY. Natural as they make 'em. (*Whispering in her ear*)
The sort of feller any girl'd love to have take her to the
races . . .

BUBBA. Races?

BARNEY (*Rushing her off her feet*). Yeh—tomorrow afternoon. Roo 'n' Olive, Pearl 'n' me, and you 'n' Johnnie! Whaddya say?

BUBBA (*Confused*). Well, I dunno. . . .

BARNEY. Oh, now, Bubba, you're not gonna be a hangout, are you? Where else can you go Sat'day afternoon?

BUBBA. N-nowhere.

BARNEY. There y'are then. Here's a chance to make whoopee . . . . How about it?
(*He eyes her anxiously. She looks timidly toward* JOHNNIE, *and then nods.*)

BUBBA. All right. If you really want me.

BARNEY (*Triumphantly*). Easy as pie, everythin' settled.

DOWD (*Dourly*). Not for me, it ain't.

BARNEY (*Turning*). Why, what else is there?

DOWD. I don't take things as easy as that. (BARNEY *opens his mouth to protest,* JOHNNIE *cuts in firmly*) You wait outside a minute—

BARNEY. But Johnnie—

DOWD. You wait outside. (BARNEY *eyes him questioningly for a second, then hunches his shoulders and moves unsteadily out to sit on front veranda. Inside,* JOHNNIE, *not so sure of his ground now, addresses himself to* BUBBA) What I mean is, I know this Barney, how he rushes people and the—the things he puts over. I want to give you a chance—you don't like the

98

idea of goin' to the races with me, you tell me now. (*He pauses, but* BUBBA *waits for further enlightenment and he is forced to stumble on*) You won't have to worry over what he'll say, I'll fix that.

BUBBA. But I'd like to go to the races.

DOWD. You looked to me as if you were holdin' back a bit.

BUBBA. It was the surprise, that's all. Roo and Barney, they've never brought anyone from up north here before.

DOWD (*Looking around*). I know. They've sat pretty tight on this joint, haven't they? D'you live here?

BUBBA. No, I'm from next door.

DOWD. Oh. That makes it a bigger hide than ever, then.

BUBBA. What?

DOWD. Him askin' you to go out with me.

BUBBA. No, it isn't. Not really. I been comin' in here a long time.

DOWD. Have yer? (*He glances over room*) Funny thing. I imagined this place pretty often. (*In answer to her puzzled look*) Oh, of course I've never been here, it's just the reputation that's been built up among the boys. I reckon you could say it's almost famous up north.

BUBBA. Things Barney said?

DOWD. Yeh. And bits of stuff the boys picked up. Or made up, by the looks of it.

(*He eyes the souvenirs disparagingly.*)

99

BUBBA (*Nervously*). It's not a—a big place.

DOWD. Size is nothin'. It's the other things—like all the fun they're supposed to have here. I just can't see it.

BUBBA (*Defensively*). You don't know.

DOWD. No? You tell me then.

BUBBA (*Turning away—shakily*). H-how can I? All that's happened in a house makes a feelin'—you can't tell anyone that. It's between people.

DOWD. Oh. (*Indicating dolls on mantelpiece*) What are the dolls in aid of?

BUBBA. Roo gives one to Olive every year when he arrives. Like a mascot.

DOWD (*Snorting in coarse amusement*). Dolls? Is that the best he can do? (BUBBA *flinches*) You didn't like me sayin' that, did you?

BUBBA. No.

DOWD. What are you, relation or somethin'? (*She shakes her head*) What's the matter then? I've hurt you some way.

BUBBA (*Turning on him*). You shouldn't have said that about the dolls. They mean somethin' to Olive and Roo, it's—it's hard to explain. You wouldn't understand it.

DOWD (*Summing up her reaction, and asking her directly one of the big questions of his life*). Tell me somethin', will yer? Why is it every time I come across anythin' connected with Roo, I'm supposed to act like I was too young to live up to it?

BUBBA (*Withdrawn, all of a sudden touched by the coincidence of their youthful insecurity*). I don't know. Maybe it's like the walkin' sticks. . . .

DOWD. The what?

BUBBA. The lolly walkin' sticks. They're a sort of present—a joke we have every year when they come down.

DOWD. Beats me. (*Abandoning the puzzle*) Anyway, what's it matter, tomorrow's the thing. That is, if you'll still come with me after the cracks I've made. Will you?

BUBBA. Yes. I'd—like to.

DOWD. What did he say your name was again?

BUBBA. Bubba Ryan.

DOWD. Bubba? Is that what they call you? (*She nods*) Seems to me they're keepin' you in the cradle, too. (*They look at one another in a moment of perfect understanding*) What's your real name?

BUBBA (*Softly*). Kathie.

DOWD. Kathie? Well, that's what I'll call you. Okay? (*He smiles at her, and she responds. Then, with a rather manufactured briskness, to prevent too sudden an entanglement*) Hey, look, at the time! I'll have to be shiftin'. (*Moves up to arch and calls*) Barney. . . . (*Warmly, to* BUBBA) We'll let him make all the arrangements, eh?

BUBBA. Try to stop him.

(BARNEY *re-enters the house from front veranda.*)

DOWD. Look, I'm goin'. I told the boys I'd be at the London by seven. Past that now.

BARNEY. Righto. You'd better say good-bye to him first. (DOWD *moves toward front door as* BARNEY *yells upstairs*) Roo—Johnnie's goin' now. (*He turns back*) Everythin' settled?

DOWD. Yeh. We're relyin' on you to fix the details.

BARNEY (*Earnestly*). You leave it to me. I'll meet you Young and Jackson's tomorrer morning half-past ten; by then I'll have it all lined up. Eh?

DOWD. Fine. (*Smiling over at* BUBBA) And you'll tell Kathie?

BARNEY. Kath . . . ? (*He follows the line of* DOWD's *gaze and realizes*) Oh yes, yes. 'Course I will. (ROO *comes downstairs, towel over his shoulder, face half-shaved*) Ah! (*He brightens mechanically*) Johnnie's got to go now, Roo.

ROO. I heard yer.

DOWD. Well, hooray, Roo, I'll see you tomorrer.

ROO. Yeh.

DOWD. Any message you want me to give the boys?

ROO. Oh . . . you know . . . just give 'em all the best.

DOWD. 'N' tell 'em to keep out of mischief, eh?
(*There is a general polite laugh,* BARNEY *claps* DOWD *on the back.*)

BARNEY. C'mon, I'll see you to the gate. (*As they move off*) You know the way back? The best thing you can do is go down to the corner; and if you don't pick up a cab by the time a tram comes, grab that, it'll take you into the city in about five minutes. . . .

> (*They have now exited.* ROO's *stare turns to* BUBBA, *who is watching* DOWD *off through the window*.)

ROO.   What are you doin' here, Bub?

BUBBA.   Barney brought me in.

ROO.   To meet him?

BUBBA.   Yes.

OLIVE (*Entering quietly to arch*).   Has he gone?

ROO.   Yeh. Made quite a picnic of it; got Bubba in to meet him, too.

OLIVE.   'Lo, darl. (*Cautiously*) Didn't seem such a bad sort of kid, really.

ROO.   Dowd? I'm not blamin' him. This is Barney's doin', he cooked this up.

OLIVE.   Well, it doesn't matter much, anyway, does it?

ROO (*Facing her with repressed anger*).   Olive, you dunno what he's done. He's forced me—brought Dowdie right into this house in the lay-off and forced me to—to knuckle under to him.

> (*He halts, unable to express his frustration.*)

OLIVE.   All right. You know best. Only don't make things any worse than they are. I've already got Emma moanin' in the kitchen, and Pearl bawlin' her eyes out upstairs. That's enough to handle—

ROO. What's wrong with Pearl?

OLIVE (*Laying tablecloth*, BUBBA *helping her*). Oh, you can't make head or tail of it. Somethin' about Barney askin' her to send her daughter to the races tomorrer—

BUBBA (*Abruptly*). He didn't ask her, he asked me.

OLIVE. To go to the races? (BUBBA *nods, and* OLIVE *laughs*) Aah —kittens! It's all fellers—Barney wouldn't take a girl to the races with a crowd of fellers. He's havin' a loan of yer.

BUBBA. He's not. And it isn't all fellers, it's just us. Us—and Johnnie.
   (OLIVE *shoots a glance at* ROO.)

ROO. Us and Johnnie? Did he tell you that?

BUBBA. Yes.

ROO. The two of them had it arranged before you came in?

BUBBA. Well, Barney asked me first, and then Johnnie—

ROO (*Seething*). As thick as thieves! (*To* OLIVE) Now d'yer see? Workin' it out between them—bloody bosom pals, that's what they are. Well, that's the finish. (*He hastily throws towel to* OLIVE *and moves toward front door, yelling*) Barney! Come in here!

OLIVE (*Following and temporizing*). Maybe they've got it all mixed up. . . .

ROO. No, they ain't. I know what his game is now. You two get out of this, down the back some place. . . .
   (BARNEY *enters from offstage and weaves his way onto*

veranda, where he pauses for a moment at the sound of the angry voices.)

BUBBA (*Frightened*). Roo . . .

OLIVE. I won't have any fightin', do you hear? Argue if you want to, but no fightin'. . . .

ROO. You stay out of it.

OLIVE. Roo . . .

ROO (*Roaring*). Get out!
(*She exits hastily with* BUBBA. BARNEY *appears in doorway.* ROO *grabs him by the lapels of his coat and hawks him inside, with a savage exclamation.*)

BARNEY. Now, easy on, Roo, I'm a bit full. . . .

ROO (*Shaking him; in a low voice of fury*). Don't you try and put that drunk stunt over on me. I know you had to have beer to get you through what you've done, but I know how much you've had. *I know!*
(*With a powerful heave, he sends* BARNEY *across the room toward mantelpiece.* BARNEY *staggers and then recovers his balance, faces* ROO. *His drunkenness drops from him like a cloak.*)

BARNEY (*White-faced*). All right. So I brought Dowdie. . . .

ROO (*Advancing*). Yes. You brought Dowdie. And don't think I dunno why.

BARNEY. For your own good.

ROO. Liar! Filthy, upjumped, rotten liar!

BARNEY (*Nettled*).   Now, let me get a word in . . .

ROO.   A man oughta cut your tongue out. (BARNEY *turns from him with disgust*) And the way you did it . . . you just had to show him how low I'd sunk, let him see me covered in stinkin' paint.

BARNEY.   What are you suddenly, a flower or somethin'? He's seen you in the fields, nearly naked, black as pitch. . . .

ROO (*Fiercely*).   Yes, and so was he. Both of us sloggin' it out under the sun! Are you tryin' to say that's the same thing as this . . . a job in a paint factory? Are you? Anyway, there's more to it than that. . . .

BARNEY (*Turns away*).   Ah, there's no use talkin' to you. . . .

ROO.   Well, you're gunna talk. Not them lies and excuses and— and lies of yours, this time we'll have it fair dinkum for once.

BARNEY (*Rounding on him*).   Righto then, here it is! You're so blind jealous of young Dowd I reckon you ought to get yourself looked at before it's too late.

ROO (*Suddenly still*).   Go on.

BARNEY (*Knowing he has gone too far but unable to retreat*). That's all. And I'm not the only one sez so!

ROO.   Who else?

BARNEY.   The boys. They weren't too pleased when you walked out on them up there, y'know. They weren't pleased at all. And I'm drummin' yer, you don't pull your socks up pretty quick, you're gunna find next season that our mob have got a new ganger for keeps.

ROO. Dowd?

BARNEY. Yeh, Dowd!

ROO (*Deceptively quiet*). And that's why you brought him here, eh? So's I could make it up with him and get back on top with the boys?

BARNEY. 'Course it is.

ROO (*Springing the trap*). Maybe you thought I could turn the trick at the races tomorrer, on a little party cooked up between you and Dowd—with Bubba as a bait!

BARNEY (*Quickly*). Oh, that. I—I was makin' a switch. . . .

ROO (*Explosively*). You was makin' a switch right enough! Your money's runnin' out, you know you can't put the bite on me any more, and so here's the new champion, all loaded and ready. And it wasn't enough to chase after him up north after I walked out on the gang, now you're aimin' to get him in here for the lay-off as well.

BARNEY (*Dangerously*). You reckon I'd work a point like that?

ROO. You'd do that and worse. 'Coz you're a slimy little leech that won't even drop off when it's got its belly full.
(BARNEY *charges him with a roar,* ROO *grapples with him whole-heartedly and swings him out onto back veranda. A confused melee of crashing pot plants, blows, and swaying ferns ensues, only part of it visible.* OLIVE *rushes in, followed by* EMMA, BUBBA *and* PEARL.)

OLIVE. Roo—stop it; stop it, Roo—

EMMA.   Keep away from them, Olive—

OLIVE (*At French windows*).   You want to murder him?

EMMA.   Pair of flamin' larrikins!

OLIVE (*Moving out of sight on veranda*).   Let him go, Roo.

EMMA.   You wanna fight, why don't you get out in the street?

OLIVE.   Roo!
(*The above lines are overlapped for the effect of agitated violence, dominated by the last screaming of* ROO's *name. He now comes back into view, breathing heavily, but unmarked.* PEARL *and* BUBBA *watch, white-faced and scared; as he moves into the room.*)

EMMA.   Lucky I didn't go straight for the cops.
(OLIVE *appears with* BARNEY. *He has obviously had the worst of the encounter.* OLIVE *assists him down to armchair, then speaks tremblingly to* ROO.)

OLIVE.   Any more of that and the two of you will sleep out in the gutter for the night. Men your age, you oughta have more sense. What do you think you're up to, anyway?

ROO (*Controlled*).   This is no business of yours, Olive. . . .

OLIVE (*Her temper stirring*).   Oh, isn't it? I'm s'posed to sit out in the back while you kick one another to pieces, I s'pose? And why? All because you had one rotten season up north.

ROO.   It ain't that at all . . .

BARNEY.   It is. (*He sways to his feet*) Why don't you be a man and admit it?

OLIVE (*Sharply*). Who wants him to admit it? It doesn't matter. . . .

BARNEY (*Inflamed*). Oh, yes, it does. Would he have walked out on his own gang if it hadn't mattered? (*To* ROO) Come on. You wanted me to be fair dinkum about Dowd, let's see you square off the same way. (ROO *is silent*) You're not game enough!

OLIVE (*Angry and puzzled*). What do you want him to say— that Dowd did a better job than he did?

BARNEY (*Straight on the nail*). Yes.

OLIVE. Righto—Roo had a bad back. Next season when he goes up, his back'll be better, and he'll beat Dowd. (BARNEY *gives a mechanical "Ha ha ha" of derision.* OLIVE *snaps*) What's so funny about that?

BARNEY (*Tauntingly*). Ask him. He'll tell you.

ROO. No, I think that's up to you. (*He charges across at* BARNEY, *pushing* OLIVE *out of the way. Savagely whips* BARNEY'S *arm up behind his back, and forces him to his knees, facing the women*) It's your lie—you tell 'em!

BARNEY (*His face contorted with pain*). Aah—cut it out. . . .

ROO (*Increasing the pressure*). Tell 'em. . . .

BARNEY (*Gasping*). He—he never had a bad back. . . .
(*Still holding him,* ROO *speaks over his head to the women, through gritted teeth.*)

ROO. Did you hear that? No strain, nothin'. Dowd did a better job than me because he's a better man than I am. That's what he wanted you to know!

(*He shoves* BARNEY *forcibly from him, and the smaller
man spins around on the floor, grasping his arm and crying out from an indefinable sense of loss and repentance.*)

BARNEY. You damned fool—do you think I would have told
them?

ROO. Well, it's about time they knew what they was dealin'
with, anyway, a coupla lousy no-hopers! (BARNEY's *head jerks
around, and* ROO's *eyes glint as he sees a weapon for revenge*)
Yeh—you, the great lover that's never had a knock back. Tell
'em how lucky you've been lately—

BARNEY (*Almost pleading*). Don't, Roo.

ROO (*Leaning down to seize him by the lapels*). This is gunna
be good! How about the two waitresses at the Greek café?

BARNEY (*Trying to twist aside to escape what is coming*). I
never went near them. . . .

ROO (*Holding him firmly*). You did, they told me. And
laughed fit to kill themselves. A fine performance that must
have been!

BARNEY. They lied about it. . . .

ROO (*Dragging him up and shaking him*). Yeh? And I s'pose
Mrs. Kelly lied when she had you thrown out of the Royal
pub? 'N' the cook at Adam's, she was lyin', and the little New
Australian woman, and Skinny Linton's missus. All of them
lyin', and you're still the best there is—like hell you are!

BARNEY (*Tearing himself free, blazing*). That's enough, Roo.

ROO *(Towering above him)*. And Nancy—after seventeen years, you couldn't even hold Nancy!

BARNEY.   You dirty rotten swine!
  (Angry beyond measure, he seizes the nearest object to his hand. It is the vase containing, among others, the seventeenth doll. This he swings at ROO's *head, but the big man rips it from his hands and throws it away into the center of the room, smashing vase and scattering dolls.* OLIVE *gives a strangled cry and* BUBBA *rushes toward her. There is a sudden silence.* OLIVE *sinks to her knees and picks up the seventeenth doll, holds it close.* BUBBA *runs up to windows and exits by back veranda. The others are unmoving.)*

Curtain

ACT THREE

ACT THREE

Time. The following morning.

The room has been tidied of all the tropical souvenirs and dolls to a neatness that gives it an oddly deserted look. In the hallway outside arch a large suitcase stands as a firm statement of imminent departure.

PEARL, dressed for outdoors in black, is standing by the window, ostensibly on the lookout for a taxi, but actually staring into space in a sad reverie. OLIVE, wearing a housecoat, enters from the arch, carrying a cup of tea, with a biscuit balanced on the saucer. PEARL turns.

OLIVE. Thought you might like a cup of tea.

PEARL. No, thanks. The taxi should be here any minute. . . .

OLIVE (*Flatly*). Half-past eight. Go on, get it down, it won't kill you. (OLIVE *is masking an immense inner dreariness with a bitter, matter-of-fact calm*) When'll you pick up the rest of your things?

PEARL. There's a taxi truck coming on Monday.

OLIVE. I'll tell Emma, she'll be home. (*Indicating room with a jerk of her head*) Notice anythin' different?

PEARL. You've cleaned the place up. I knew you was doin' it. I heard you after I'd gone to bed.

OLIVE. Didn't mean to, y'know. I started off tryin' to fix up what they broke. After that I couldn't seem to stop. (*She laughs mirthlessly*) Emma always sez tryin' to shift heavy furniture on your own's a sign you're crooked on the world. Wonder what spring cleanin' at two o'clock in the mornin' means? (PEARL *makes no comment*) Just you don't want to go to bed, I s'pose.

PEARL (*Indirectly*).   When d'you expect Barney back?

OLIVE.   Can't tell. The way he slammed out of here last night, he could have been headin' straight for Cairns. But if I know him, he'll be back before the day's out.

PEARL.   If you know him. Somehow, Olive, I don't think you do.

OLIVE.   After seventeen years?

PEARL.   All the time you talk about years—how long you've been doin' this—how long you've been goin' there—and what does it prove? Nothin'. There's not one thing I've found here been anythin' like what you told me.

OLIVE (*Tiredly*).   Oh, Pearl.

PEARL.   No "oh, Pearl" about it. Last night, when I couldn't sleep, I figured out what's the matter with you. You're blind to everythin' outside this house and the lay-off season.

OLIVE.   I'm blind to what I want to be.

PEARL.   All right. But the least you can do is to see what you've got as it really is. Take a look at this place now you've pulled down the decorations—what's so wonderful about it? Nothin'! It's just an ordinary little room that's a hell of a lot the worse for wear. And if you'd only come out of your daydream long enough to take a grown-up look at the lay-off, that's what you'd find with the rest of it.

OLIVE (*Steelily*).   Listen, I'm gunna say this just once. All I told you about Roo and Barney and their time here was Gospel true—I'll swear it—for every year up until now. And if it hasn't been true for this year, maybe you're the last should be squealin' about it.

PEARL (*Her eyes widening*).   You're blamin' me, aren't you? Because I was here instead of Nancy.

OLIVE.   Yes.
(BARNEY *enters from offstage, crosses front veranda.*)

PEARL.   I'm wastin' my breath, then. If you can't see further than that, I'm just wastin' my breath.
(BARNEY *knocks at front door.*)

OLIVE (*Stiffly*).   That'll be your taxi. . . . (*Looks through window*) No it's not, it's Barney.
(*She makes a move for arch, but* PEARL *checks her.*)

PEARL.   You're not gunna let him in.

OLIVE.   Why not?

PEARL.   He'll only try to talk me 'round.

OLIVE (*With a shade of relish*).   We'll see who knows him best, you or me. (PEARL *sits erect and uncompromising.* OLIVE *opens the front door and* BARNEY *enters*) Well, wherever it was, they certainly threw you out early.

BARNEY.   Yeh.
(*He enters into hallway and stops before case.* OLIVE *speaks, shutting door.*)

OLIVE.   You're just in time to say good-bye to Pearl.

BARNEY (*Impersonally*).   I thought she'd be goin'. (*As he tosses his coat on to sideboard he sights* PEARL) Oh—'lo, Pearlie.

PEARL (*Huskily*).   Hello.

OLIVE (*Cuttingly*).   I don't wanna spoil anythin', and, besides, I haven't had me breakfast. In the kitchen if you want me.
>   (*She exits. There is a pause, tense on* PEARL'S *part, flat on* BARNEY'S. *He is staring at the suitcase, and finally touches it with his foot.*)

BARNEY.   You thinkin' of carryin' this somewhere?

PEARL (*Strained*).   There's a taxi comin'. . . .

BARNEY.   Oh. I was gunna say, you'd better let me give you a hand. A thing that size, no job for a woman.
>   (*He wanders away from her.* PEARL *watches him, then blurts out without thinking.*)

PEARL.   Where've you been to?

BARNEY.   Eh? (*He comes out of his abstraction to look at her, and laughs, shaking his head*) Oh, no, fair go, that's the question for a missus. And you're leavin', remember! (*She turns away, embarrassed, and he appraises her clothes*) 'Struth, I'll bet that's the most respectable get-up in the whole of your wardrobe. I don't mind you walkin' out on me, luvvie, but do you have to look as if you're leavin' a corpse?

PEARL (*Putting on gloves*).   I knew you wouldn't be able to stand the thought of me bein' respectable again.

BARNEY.   Pearlie, I'll let you into a secret. You've never been anythin' else.

PEARL (*Flashing*). Maybe I haven't been any second Nancy, but then I never set out to be.

BARNEY (*Puzzled*). Why the hell pick on poor old Nance? (*She maintains a tight-lipped silence*) If it comes to that, you're walkin' out for the very same reason she did.

PEARL. Nancy left to get married.

BARNEY. Only because she couldn't get what she wanted here.

PEARL (*In sad exasperation*). You can still see yourself as the biggest prize in the packet, can't you? Well, I might have had some idea when I came into this of turnin' it into a—a little peace and security for myself. Yes, marryin' you. I was silly enough to have thought it would have worked out. But not after last night. And it isn't only findin' out you're the great has-been. It's what you wanted me to do with Vera.

BARNEY. She was asked to the races. One afternoon.

PEARL. Yeh, and I know what sort of runnin' goes on! I got caught up in it myself round her age, and I've ended up here with you. Well, it's not gunna happen to my daughter. She's gunna have the sort of respectability that doesn't need a black dress to show it.

BARNEY. All right, Pearl, all right. You go ahead and become the strictest motherin' barmaid in the business. I'm not tryin' to stop you.
(*A slight pause, then she asks on a note of reluctant curiosity—*)

PEARL. There's just one thing I would like to know. . . .

BARNEY. What? (*There is the noise of a car pulling up offstage, and a horn sounds*) There's your taxi. (*He yells through window*) Goodo, sport, be with you in a minute. (*He turns back to* PEARL) What was it you wanted to know?

PEARL. That first mornin' you—you said there was three things a woman needed to have. You never told me what the third one was.

BARNEY. Don't you think it's a bit late for that now? And you haven't got it, anyway. (*Her lip quivers at the rebuff*) Oh, don't let it worry you. I've only ever met one woman who had.

PEARL (*Quietly*). Nancy.

BARNEY. Yeh. (*Wryly*) And even she didn't have enough to keep the two of us together. I'll carry your bag out.
(*He picks up her case as* OLIVE *enters.*)

OLIVE. That the taxi?

BARNEY. Yeh.
(*He moves out with suitcase, and during the following he crosses the veranda to exit offstage.* PEARL *goes up to hallway.*)

OLIVE (*Reserved*). Well—see you Monday then, will I?

PEARL. Yeh. And you'll tell Clintie. . . .

OLIVE. You've got a headache and won't be in today. I know.
(PEARL *hesitates and then, a little clumsily, speaks softly.*)

PEARL. I'm sorry, Olive. I wasn't the type, that's all.
(*She exits.* OLIVE *moves to front door to watch her departure.* ROO *enters down stairs.*)

ROO (*Gruffly*). 'S that Pearl goin'?

OLIVE. Yes. Barney's seein' her off.

ROO. Oh. He's back, is he?

OLIVE. I said so, didn't I?
  (*Taxi starts up offstage and drives away.* OLIVE *closes the door.*)

ROO (*Eyeing room over*). You've taken down the dolls and all that other stuff.

OLIVE. Last night. (*She catches his reproachful glance, and says in irritation*) Oh, it's not just because you gave them to me. I took 'em down to dust, and those birds and butterflies, they just fell to pieces. You couldn't even touch them. Then the rest of it—well, some of the dolls were broken, and the shells looked so silly on their own, I just couldn't put them back.

ROO. I'll get you some new ones.

OLIVE. No, you won't. Plenty to waste your time on besides chasin' those things.

ROO. You always said you liked 'em.

OLIVE. I used to like a lot of things I ain't seen much of lately. A bit of a joke and a laugh, for instance. If I can do without that, I won't miss a few bloomin'—decorations.

ROO. Olive, that stoush had been brewin' for a long time. And you saw what Barney did to me.

OLIVE (*Challenging him*). What? He got full and brought home some bloke you don't like. That's all I saw.

ROO (*Another of his vain struggles for the right word*). Nobody—nobody else in the gang would have—ah—what's the use? (*A pause, then he speaks distantly*) All I know is shakin' hands with Dowd last night was the hardest thing I've ever done in my life. And when I walked out of this room there was no feelin' in my fingers (*He flexes them*) . . . like they'd been crushed or somethin'. (*Staring at his hands*) That's just how it was—like they'd been crushed.

OLIVE. Righto, so it means a lot to all of you up north. But why the hell couldn't you leave it up there? It's got nothin' to do with our time down here, has it? Did you have to smash that up as well?

ROO (*Turning to her, sensing she is near tears*). I didn't mean to. Honest, Ol, that's one thing just seemed to happen.

OLIVE. It happened, all right. (*She whirls up to arch just in time to meet* EMMA *making an entrance*) And what do you want? Can't you hear enough from the kitchen?

EMMA (*Indignantly*). I wasn't listenin'. I came up to get that cup and saucer.

OLIVE. Yeh. I'll bet.
(*She exits upstairs.* EMMA *gives an "Oh" of pretended affront.*)

EMMA (*Coming into room and picking up cup on table*). She's got a nasty mind, that Olive. Bad enough to have to trail around pickin' up after her, but when she insults you for it . . . (*Looks at* ROO, *who is staring moodily at the floor*) Here, you're not gunna let her get you down, are yer?

ROO. So you was listenin'.

EMMA. 'Course I was. I told you, it's the only way I can find
out anythin'. And a mornin' like this, wouldn't miss it for all
the tea in China. (*She relaxes enjoyably*) This is what I call
interestin'. The lot of yez squabbling at last 'stead of all that
playin' around went on other times. Only thing I'm sorry for
is Nancy ain't here. She knew which way the wind was
blowin', that one.

ROO (*Slowly*).   Nancy got married.

EMMA.   Nancy got out while the goin' was good, that's what
Nancy did.

ROO.   You think you know all about it, don't yer?

EMMA.   I been 'round here long enough, ain't I? I bet I can tell
you things you don't even remember. Like that first Sunday
when they met yez at the Aquarium, and Nancy made that
crack about youse and the fish. Remember?

ROO.   Somethin' about bein' out of our depths, wasn't it?

EMMA.   No. Thousands of fish all swimmin' in their tanks, but
yez was the only two out of water. Real wag. I liked Nance.

ROO.   I reckon we all did.

EMMA.   Shrewd, though. She could buy and sell Olive.

ROO.   I never noticed her shrewd.

EMMA.   Oh, she was. She was.

ROO (*In sudden resolve*).   C'mon, Emma, you're supposed to
know the lot. Whose fault do you reckon it was—mine or Barney's?

EMMA. What fault?

ROO. Oh, I don't just mean the blue last night—who's to blame for messin' up the whole thing?

EMMA. You're kiddin', aren't yer?

ROO. No, fair dinkum, I want to know.

EMMA. Well, I'll be blowed! (*She looks at him in astonishment*) How long did you think these lay-off seasons were gunna last—forever? They're not for keeps, you know; these are just—seasons.

ROO. I know, but whose fault was it we come a cropper?

EMMA. Nobody's fault, yer melon!

ROO. Don't be silly, it must be somebody's. . . .

EMMA (*Exasperated*). Why must it? All that's happened is you've gone as far as you can go. You 'n' Barney 'n' Olive, you're too old for it any more.

ROO. Old?

EMMA. That's it—old! Take a look in the mirror.

ROO. Nobody tells me I'm old. I'm as good a man now as ever I was.

EMMA. Are yer? Then who the hell was that bloke Barney brought here last night? A mirage or somethin'?

ROO (*Stubbornly*). I ain't old! Old is—what you are, and—and—(*He gropes for a name and the one he eventually finds is a shock to him*)—Tony Moreno.

(After a moment he turns to survey his face questioningly in the mirror over the mantel. It is the action of doubt. From here on ROO *is at the mercy of an entirely different conception of himself.)*

EMMA.   I didn't mean you was up for the pension. But you ain't seventeen any more, either. Look, sit down a minute. . . . *(He refuses with a dogged shake of the head. She says curiously)* Strikes me you don't know what's hit you, do you?

ROO.   All I know is somethin' went wrong, and I reckon it was Barney.

EMMA.   Well, maybe Barney had a bit more to do with it than you did, but he's been slippin' longer than you have, don't forget that. . . .

ROO *(Strongly)*.   I ain't slipped. Never you say that. What I had was one lousy season.

EMMA.   So far. That's the first.

ROO.   You think there could be another bad as that?

EMMA.   Lots of them. Don't you?

ROO *(On a rising note)*.   You reckon I can't even earn a livin' any more?

EMMA.   Yes, you can still earn a livin'. But that's not what we're talkin' about, is it? *(There is a pause while he turns away from her. When he is still, she speaks)* Why do you think Barney lied about your back?

ROO.   Lyin' comes as natural to him as skittin'.

125

EMMA. Not always, it didn't. You listen—before Barney started to get the brushoff from women, he only skited. Now he lies. Work it out for yourself. When did he start lyin' about you? Eh? (*He is dumb, and she rises, bridling a little*) Yeh, I might be a damned old fool around the place, but I can still nut that one out. You and Barney are two of a pair. Only the time he spent chasin' wimmen, you put in bein' top dog! Well, that's all very fine and a lot of fun while it lasts, but last is one thing it just don't do. There's a time for sowin' and a time for reapin'—and reapin' is what you're doin' now.

> (*She moves to pick up cup and saucer, clearly intending to leave the room, but he stays her with a tired gesture, visualizing his defeat for the first time.*)

ROO. Hang on, Emma. (*He draws a deep breath*) I dunno . . . maybe you're talkin' sense.

EMMA. I am. 'N' if you'd had half an eye between yez, you would have seen what you was headin' for long ago.

ROO. I s'pose we would. Nobody stopped to look, that's all.

EMMA. Nancy did. And now it's time for the rest of yez.

ROO. What about Olive?

EMMA. Olive? Olive's a fool. I'll show you somethin'. (*She puts cup and saucer on sideboard, rummages in cupboard underneath, and drags out the seventeenth doll. She speaks with bitterness*) You see this? Middle of the night Olive sat here on the floor, huggin' this and howlin'. A grown-up woman, howlin' over a silly old kewpie doll. That's Olive for yer!

> (*She tosses doll onto table, takes cup and saucer, and moves towards kitchen. In the hallway she hesitates, how-*

ever, places cup and saucer on hall table and goes upstairs to OLIVE. ROO *stands, dazed with misery, then makes his way to pick up doll and smooth its fuzzy skirts.* BARNEY'S *voice is heard commandingly off—"Bubba!" and she is heard to reply, "You leave me alone."* BUBBA *appears in windows at back veranda, followed by* BARNEY. *He seizes her arm as if to expostulate with her, but she drags herself free of him.* ROO *puts doll aside on piano top.*)

BUBBA.   Let me go!

BARNEY.   Don't be a fool! What difference will talkin' to Olive make?

BUBBA.   She'll tell me whether it's true or not.

BARNEY.   Why wouldn't it be?
(*They are both now in the room.*)

ROO.   What is it?

BUBBA.   Barney came and told me that the—the races are off.

BARNEY.   I didn't. I said that I'm goin' and the boys are goin', but you're not, and—nobody else is.

ROO.   That's right, Bub.

BARNEY.   I fixed it at the Stadium last night. Told Dowdie you couldn't come.

BUBBA.   Did you? Well, now I'll go down and tell him that I can come. Where's he stayin'?

BARNEY.   Bubba, there's a big crowd of fellers livin' with him.
    • • •

BUBBA. I don't care. You tell me where he is or I'll be waitin' outside Young and Jackson's when you go down to meet him half-past ten.

BARNEY. I'm not meetin' him Young and Jackson's. . . .

BUBBA. You are. I heard you fix it with him last night.
(BARNEY *is helpless before the thrust of her vehemence, and* ROO *interrupts.*)

ROO. Now, just a moment, Bubba. . . .

BUBBA. It's no use tryin' to talk me out of it, Roo.

ROO. Far as I'm concerned, you can go down and see him any time you want to. But first I reckon you oughta know the reason why you was asked to the races.

BARNEY. It was me. I was drunk!

BUBBA. You weren't the one that asked me—he did!

BARNEY. Didn't I go into your place and get you?

BUBBA. Yes, but he asked me. He sent you out of the room and told me not to—to take any notice of what you said. Then he asked me. . . .

ROO. Bubba, Dowd had been drinkin' as well. The pair of them. By this mornin' he's probably forgotten he ever met you. . . .

BARNEY. Would you risk goin' down there and havin' him make a fool of you in front of all those other fellers?

ROO. Would you, Bubba?
(*She is silent.* ROO's *question forces an answer from her.*)

BUBBA. Yes.

BARNEY (*Amazed*). Well, what the hell's so important about goin' to the races?

BUBBA. He asked me.

BARNEY. I know, but even if he did . . .

BUBBA. He asked me! And he didn't call me B-Bubba or kid, he wanted to know what my real name was, and when I told him, that's what he called me. Kathie. (*She turns away to* ROO) He might have been drinkin', and this mornin' he might have forgotten, like you said, but this is the only chance I've ever had of comin' close to—I dunno—whatever it is I've been watchin' all these years. You think I'll give that up?

BARNEY. Bubba, you don't know this Johnnie Dowd He's not like me or Roo. . . .

BUBBA. He is!

BARNEY. You don't know him.

BUBBA. He's more like you than—than they are.

BARNEY. Who?

BUBBA (*Wildly*). The others! Any of the fellers I've ever met down here.

BARNEY (*Viciously determined to disillusion her*). Who d'yer think caused that fight last night?

ROO (*Swiftly*). No, you hold on. The fight hadn't anythin' to do with this. (*He pauses*) Bubba, come over here. (*He is sitting on piano stool. She goes to him, and he puts out his hand for her to take*) You're sure you know what it is you're after?

BUBBA. Yes.

(*She kneels impulsively before him.*)

ROO (*Searchingly*). We've spoilt it for you, ain't we? A long time.

BUBBA. Not spoilt—it's—it's just that nothin' else is any good, that's all.

ROO. Even after what you saw last night.

BUBBA. That won't happen to me.

ROO. How can you be sure, Bub?

BUBBA. Because I won't let it! Dolls and breakin' things, and —and arguments about who was best—what do they all matter? That wasn't the lay-off.

ROO. It's what it came to.

BUBBA (*Rising and dragging her hands away from him*). Well, it won't for me. I'll have what you had—the real part of it— but I'll have it differently. Some way I can have it safe and know that it's goin' to last.

ROO (*Softly*). Little Bubba—you've outgrown the lot of us, haven't you?

BUBBA (*Now uncertain of herself*). I—I hadn't thought of it that way, but I s'pose I have.

(ROO *rises and looks toward* BARNEY.)

ROO. Tell her where he's puttin' up.

BARNEY (*After a pause, and not very graciously*). The Coffee Palace. (*As she hugs* ROO) And he's goin' away Monday.

ROO. Never mind that. (*To* BUBBA, *as she moves*) Now don't you go down there in front of all them fellers. You ring him up and arrange to meet him somewhere. D'you hear me?

BUBBA. All right.

ROO. 'N' don't make yourself cheap. Tell him you're ringin' because you can't get any sense out of Barney.

BUBBA. Yes. (*She moves over to* BARNEY, *who is scowling over* ROO's *last remark, and she asks, a little timidly*) Are you mad at me for messin' up your day?
(*He shrugs it off.*)

BARNEY. Aw, what's a day? I can still meet up with the rest of 'em. You go ahead. (*Kisses her cheek*) All the best, Bub.
(*She moves to French windows and looks back at them, eyes glistening.*)

BUBBA. You don't have to worry about me—honest—I'll be all right.

ROO. Yeh, we know—Kathie.
(*She turns and runs over back veranda to exit.* BARNEY *moves up to look after her.*)

BARNEY. If he doesn't treat her right I'll kick his inside out.

ROO. Yeh.
(BARNEY *hesitates a second, then moves in for the plunge.*)

BARNEY. Look, we might as well get this straight while we're at it. The mob is pullin' out on Monday—up the Murray for the grapes. I'm goin' with them.

ROO (*Nodding*). With Dowd.

BARNEY. There's a crowd of us goin'.

ROO (*Quietly*). You're goin' with Dowd.

BARNEY (*Impatiently*). All right then, I'm goin' with Dowd. You want to make anythin' out of it?

ROO. Why should I? I don't bloody care any more.

BARNEY (*Arrested, rather shocked*). That fixes that, then. (*Trying to regain defiance*) And I tell yer, it's not just that me money's runnin' out, either. Last night was the finish for my books. We're poison to each other now. I reckon the only way out for both of us is to split up for a while.

ROO. Maybe it is.

BARNEY. I'll go up the Murray with them, and you can stay down here. That'll make a change for the two of us. Then, when the season comes on again, we can all meet up north— and who knows, we might be able to give it another burl. Whaddya say?

ROO (*In slow conviction*). Only one thing wrong with that.

BARNEY. What?

ROO. I ain't goin' up for the season.

BARNEY (*Thunderstruck*). You're not? Where you goin' then?

ROO. Nowhere. I'm stayin' here.

BARNEY. For the winter? You're crazy.

ROO. It won't be so bad. . . .

BARNEY.   Bad, me foot. You're talkin' about winter, remember.

ROO.   Olive lives through it. Millions of people do.

BARNEY (*Forcibly*).   They was born here! You've lived in the sun all your life.

ROO.   Time I made a change then.
(*He is lighting a cigarette.*)

BARNEY.   But why? What the hell's the matter with the sun?

ROO (*Deeply*).   Nothin'. (*Staring at the tiny flame of the match*) The sun's great. It's just I—I've had too much of a good thing, that's all.
(*He gently blows out the light.*)

BARNEY (*Mystified*).   Well, you're a beaut. Honest, I dunno what to make of you. It's like—like you was cuttin' off your nose to spite your face. Only you don't sound mad about it. (*Trying a new tack*) It wouldn't be anythin' on account of Bubba, would it?

ROO (*Passively*).   No. Nothin' on account of Bubba.
(*A pause.* BARNEY *is staring at* ROO, *trying to unravel the puzzle. From upstairs* EMMA'S *voice raises a distant thread of indistinct rancor.*)

EMMA (*Off*).   Why don't you ring them?

OLIVE (*Coming downstairs*).   I don't wanna.

EMMA (*Following—a last jibe*).   No, you wouldn't.
(*She goes off toward kitchen, having collected cup from hall table.* OLIVE *appears in the arch, dressed for the street.* ROO *and* BARNEY, *whose attention has been caught by the*

above exchange, register her appearance with as much imperturbability as they can muster. OLIVE's *mood is difficult and strained.*)

OLIVE (*Coming into the room*).   The two great bruisers! You can bear to be together in the same room again, can you?

BARNEY.   We was workin' out the damage.

OLIVE.   Well, that shouldn't take you long. An old cracked vase and some decorations. Hardly worth your while, really.

BARNEY.   We was takin' it a bit further than that. . . .

OLIVE.   How? Tatty decorations was all you had left to break. The rest went months ago.

ROO (*In half-shamed remonstrance*).   Olive!

OLIVE.   Olive nothing!

BARNEY.   The Sat'day-morning sulks, eh?

OLIVE.   Yeh. Does it surprise you?

BARNEY.   Not much. But don't get it into your head you're the only one losin 'out over this bust-up. There's Roo and me, too, you know.

OLIVE (*Satirically*).   What have you lost—Pearl?

ROO.   We don't have to have any more of that. . . .

BARNEY (*Overlapping* ROO's *last words*).   I didn't mind Pearl. . . . If I hadn't been leavin' on Monday. . . .

ROO (*Commandingly*).   Barney! (BARNEY *cuts short.* OLIVE's *eyes dart to* ROO *as he speaks*) You've got some packin' to do, haven't you?

(BARNEY *pauses, offended, nods shortly and moves to exit.*)

OLIVE (*Savoring it*).   Monday! Oh, no wonder you were lookin' over the damage. . . .

ROO.   Olive, I wanna talk to you. . . .

OLIVE.   I'll bet. Settlin'-up time already, is it? Well, make me an offer—vase, decorations, and everythin' else you've smashed —how much?

ROO.   Now, just a minute. . . .

OLIVE.   This is where I collect, ain't it? In cold hard cash, Roo —seventeen summers—what are they worth?

ROO (*Incensed*).   Will you stop your bitchin' long enough for me to tell you somethin'? Barney's the one that's goin' Monday, not me. I'm stayin' right here. (*This quietens her, and he adds disgustedly*) Talkin' money that way. It's rotten!

OLIVE.   I forgot. You're the sort likes to leave it on the mantelpiece under the clock, aren't you.

ROO (*Shocked and restrained*).   Now look, Olive, that's enough. I know you've 'ad a bad spin and I know you're all on edge, but we've never been as low and cheap as that, ever.

OLIVE.   Well, we are now. Low and cheap's just how I feel.

ROO.   Because of me?

OLIVE.   You, Barney, the whole damned season. Even Pearl, the way she looked at me this mornin' when she told me I—I didn't know what livin' was.

ROO. That's a fine thing to let worry you, the way Pearl looks—

OLIVE. You didn't see her. And it's more than lookin' (*This is difficult for her to say*)—it's havin' another woman walkin' around knowin' your inside and sorry for you 'coz she thinks you've never been within cooee of the real thing. That's what hurts. (*Her control gives way and she starts to cry. At first she tries to dam the tears, resulting in a choked whimper, but when* ROO *says with infinite love and pity,* "Oh, hon," *and moves toward her, the floodgates are opened*) It was all true, everythin' I told her was true, an'—an' she didn't see any of it.

ROO. Hon, don't cry now, you couldn't help it. . . .

OLIVE. B-but if she could have seen just a little bit, so she'd know. . . .

ROO. Maybe she did.

OLIVE (*Breaking from him and collapsing into armchair*). No, no, she didn't. It was all different. . . .
　　(*She bursts into hopeless sobs.*)

ROO (*Awkwardly sitting on edge of chair*). Well, that old Pearlie, she couldn't tell anyway, this isn't her cup of tea. Stop your cryin' now. (*He puts his arms around her*) We'll just forget that she ever came here.

OLIVE. Y-yes. (*She leans against him for a moment and he kisses her hair. Then she struggles up, sniffing*) I—I ought to have a hankie somewhere. . . .
　　(*She fishes about and finds one in her sleeve, blows her nose sensibly and dabs her eyes.*)

ROO (*In teasing warmth*). I never knew any cryin' woman look worse than you do.

OLIVE. It's 'coz I cry so—so hard. (*She gulps and dabs at her eyes again before saying repentantly*) Roo . . .

ROO. What?

OLIVE. Those butterflies, they—they did fall to pieces when I touched them. . . .

ROO. I believe you.

OLIVE. But the dolls, I could've put them back. Only I was mad at you, and I wouldn't. . . .

ROO. Doesn't matter.

OLIVE. Yes, it does. I'll do it after. And—and I might be able to get the birds fixed up a bit.

ROO (*Softly*). Y'know, a man's a fool to treat you as a woman. You're nothin' but a little girl about twelve years old.

OLIVE. T-try tellin' that to the mob on a Saturday night.

ROO. 'S true, just the same. (*They kiss gently*) Have you really got to go to the pub today?

OLIVE. Yes, I ought to. . . .

ROO (*Rising*). Take the day off, and we'll go for a picnic, just the two of us. . . .

OLIVE. I'd like to, but there's Pearl away already and I said I'd sling a line to Clintie for her. I just know what I must look like. (*She goes to her bag at mantelpiece. As she fumbles with the catch she says more brightly*) Why don't you and Barney come down for the afternoon?

ROO. He's going to the races with the boys.

OLIVE. Oh. (*Inspecting damage in her purse-flap mirror*) Talk about the wreck of the *Hesprus*. (*Fishing for cosmetics*) Is it the boys he's nickin' off with on Monday?

ROO. Yeh. Up the Murray for the grapes.

OLIVE (*Diverted from her search for a moment*). It'll be funny without Barney around. Can't you get him to stay?

ROO (*Negatively*). He won't take a job in the city.

OLIVE. Well, I don't blame him for that. (ROO *reacts stiffly. Moving slowly towards him, she inquires somewhat nervously*) Would you like to—to go up the Murray with him?

ROO. No.

OLIVE (*Not looking at him*). 'Coz if you would—I mean, I wouldn't mind it for just this once.

ROO. Are you tryin' to get rid of me?

OLIVE. No, but other times you've always left together; it doesn't seem right. . . .

ROO. Olive, I'm stayin' here with you.

OLIVE (*Staring at him now*). Well—how will you meet up together for the season?

ROO. Say we don't? Barney'll get along, he doesn't need me any more, he knows plenty of fellers. And this young Dowd, it looks like they're gunna team up together.

OLIVE. But you, Roo—what'll happen to you?

ROO. Nothin'. I'm not goin' back, Olive. Not for this season or —or any other. (*He moves in to take her stiffened, bewildered*

body into his arms) Let me get rid of this for a moment. . . .
(*He takes the handbag from her unresisting fingers and drops it on the table.*)

OLIVE (*Almost whispering*). You're not goin' back?

ROO (*Tenderly*). Look, I know this is seventeen years too late, and what I'm offerin' is not much chop, but—I want to marry you, Ol.
(*There is a moment of frozen horror, and then she pushes herself away from him, almost screaming with quivering intensity.*)

OLIVE. No!

ROO. Olive . . .

OLIVE. You can't get out of it like that—I won't let you. . . .

ROO (*Appalled*). Olive, what the hell's wrong?

OLIVE. You've got to go back. It's the only hope we've got. . . .

ROO. Stop that screamin', will yer. . . .

OLIVE. You think I'll let it all end up in marriage—every day—a paint factory—you think I'll marry you?

ROO (*Grabbing her and shouting back*). What else can we do? You gone mad or somethin'? First you tell me I've made you low, and now look—you dunno what you want!

OLIVE (*Breaking away, possessed*). I do—I want what I had before. (*She rushes at him and pummels his chest*) You give it back to me—give me back what you've taken. . . .

ROO (*Grabbing her wrists and holding them tight*). Olive, it's gone—can't you understand? Every last little scrap of it—gone!

(*He throws her away from him, and she falls to the floor, grief-stricken, almost an animal in her sense of loss.*)

OLIVE. I won't let you—I'll kill you first!

ROO (*Lashing at her, hurting himself at the same time*). Kill me, then. But there's no more flyin' down out of the sun—no more birds of paradise. . . . (*Going down on one knee beside her and striking the floor with his hand*) This is the dust we're in and we're gunna walk through it like everyone else for the rest of our lives!

(*She gives a rasping cry and doubles over herself on the floor, as if cradling an awful inner pain. ROO kneels watching her, his breath coming in gasps. EMMA comes quickly in from the kitchen as BARNEY'S voice is heard calling in apprehension from upstairs.*)

BARNEY (*Off*). What's goin' on down there?

(*He comes hastily downstairs and into the room. EMMA meanwhile has come to crouch beside OLIVE.*)

EMMA. Olive . . .

ROO (*Backing away, choked*). Give it back to me, she says. As if I'd taken it away from her—me.

EMMA. Olly, what's the matter? Tell me. (*But OLIVE shakes her head dumbly, not looking up. She draws away from her mother and rises, swaying. Lifts her head to stare at ROO, his whole bearing one of uncompromising rejection. There is an unbelieving moment, then she stumbles forward to pick up her bag and move from the house. It is the progress of a drunk woman, her head hangs down, her hair is tumbled about her face, and she lurches as she walks. The only sound is a rhyth-*

mic gagging catch in the throat, too elemental to be defined as sobbing. On the veranda, she steadies herself for a moment against a post, clinging for support before relinquishing her grip to plunge off front veranda and wander away out of sight. After a pause EMMA *rises and moves up to arch. With low, grim determination*) There's nothin' you can do for her now—except to clear out and never come back. The lay-offs in this house are finished—for all of you.

(*She turns and exits to the kitchen, suddenly seeming a worn-out, old, shambling woman.* BARNEY *stares after her for a second, then looks at* ROO, *standing immobile by the table.* BARNEY *makes a decision and begins quietly, but with tremendous purpose.*)

BARNEY.   To hell with Dowd! To hell with all the boys! They can pick grapes or do anythin' they want to, I won't even get in touch with them. We'll go off on our own, Roo, we'll make a fresh start. There's plenty of places we can go to—that bloke up in Warwick, he's always said he'd give us a job any time we ever wanted one. (ROO *moves toward window to look after* OLIVE) Or even—look, we don't have to go any place we've ever been before, even. How about that, Roo? We've been goin' to the same places for so long and doin' the same things that we've started to run ourselves into the ground. That's what's wrong with us! (*Coming behind* ROO) And there's a whole bloody country out there—wide open before us. (ROO's *gaze fixes on the seventeenth doll on top of the piano*) There's all the West—we can hit Perth, and then work our way right through up to Broome there. Or even—(Roo, *breathing heavily, picks up the doll.* BARNEY, *knowing he has failed, carries on in a desperate rising tone, but backing away from the wrath he senses is to come*) Look, Roo, this is even better.

That Rum Jungle you hear so much about! There's a packet in it, they reckon. I bet fellers like us could really clean up there—and we wouldn't have to give a Continental for—(*He breaks off as* ROO, *in a baffled insensate rage, begins to beat the doll down and down again on the piano, smashing and tearing at it until it is nothing but a litter of broken cane, tinsel and celluloid. Only when it is in this state does it drop from his hands, leaving one torn shred of silk caught between his fingers. His body sags as the tremendous energy sustaining him through this last effort starts to drain away. Swaying a little on his feet like a beaten bull, he slowly folds down onto the piano stool and buries his face in his hands. Something breaks deep within him, but there is no movement in his body, he is far too inarticulate for the release of tears. After a pause,* BARNEY, *with a wisdom that momentarily transcends his usual shallow self, comes in slowly to put his hands on the big man's shoulders*) Come on, Roo. Come on, boy.

(*He pats the shoulder under his hands once, comfortingly, then moves up to collect his coat, sling it over his back, and stand waiting.* ROO *comes out of his collapse and the shred of silk between his fingers takes his attention. Rises, staring at it in a helpless sort of anguished misery, then opens his fingers to let it flutter down to the rest of the mess on the floor. Looks across at* BARNEY, *and in this brief meeting of eyes there is no bravado or questing hope, it is a completely open acknowledgment of what they have lost.* BARNEY *jerks his head, indicating the open front door, and as* ROO *starts to move up to join him,*

The Curtain Falls